JEFFERSON COUNTY TENNESSEE
Minute Books
1782 thru 1816
Index

Transcribed by
Wayne Shaw

a & b - assault & battery
adm - administrator
b.o.s. - bill of sale
def - defendent
est - estate
exr - executor
f.a.b. - felonious assault & battery
guard - guardian
mark - mark & brand
ng - not given
p.o.a - power of attorney
plt - plaintiff

/ = of
[ ] = age of individual

JEFFERSON COUNTY TENNESSEE COURT MINUTE BOOKS
INDEX 1783-1816

LAST	FIRST	MON	YEAR	PAGE	OTHER
Adams	Daniel		1792	9	juror
Adams	George	8	1795	49	juror
Adams	George	5	1796	57	plt
Adams	William		1792	9	juror
Adams	William		1792	17	juror
Adams	William	5	1794	28	def
Adams	Wm	8	1794	34	juror
Adams	Wm	2	1795	36	plt
Adams	Wm	5	1795	44	juror
Adams	Wm	5	1795	46	juror
Adams	Wm	8	1795	49	def
Adams	Wm	5	1796	57	plt
Adams	Wm	11	1797	93	plt
Albertson	Early	10	1798	127	juror
Aldman	Thomas	8	1795	48	juror
Alexander	James		1792	24	juror
Alexander	James	5	1794	25	juror
Alexander	James	5	1794	27	juror
Alexander	James	2	1795	38	juror
Alexander	James	8	1795	48	juror
Alexander	James	5	1796	57	juror
Alexander	James	5	1796	58	juror
Alexander	James	5	1796	62	juror
Alexander	James	8	1796	63	juror
Alexander	Joseph		1792	13	juror
Alexander	Joseph		1792	21	juror
Alexander	Joseph	5	1795	45	juror
Alexander	Joseph	8	1795	50	juror
Allen	Ben	7	1798	122	juror
Allen	Ben	7	1798	123	juror
Allen	Benjamin	5	1796	62	plt
Allen	Isaac		1792	6	juror
Allen	John	1	1798	116	def
Allen	John	1	1798	116	def
Allen	John	7	1798	121	def
Allen	Solomon	5	1796	60	juror
Allen	William		1792	2	trespass
Allen	William		1792	3	
Allen	William		1792	4	plt

JEFFERSON COUNTY TENNESSEE COURT MINUTE BOOKS
INDEX 1783-1816

LAST	FIRST	MON	YEAR	PAGE	OTHER
Alt	John	1	1798	111	juror
Alt	John	1	1798	112	juror
Anderson	Barnabas	1	1799	134	plt
Anderson	John		1792	7	juror
Anderson	John		1792	11	affray
Anderson	John		1792	14	juror
Anderson	John		1792	15	juror
Anderson	John		1792	22	juror
Anderson	Joseph	7	1799	150	def
Armstrong	Alexander		1792	20	juror
Armstrong	John	4	1798	118	plt
Arthur	Thomas		1792	18	juror
Arthur	Thomas	5	1794	25	juror
Arthur	Thomas	5	1794	27	def
Arthur	Thomas	5	1794	28	juror
Arthur	Thomas	8	1794	33	juror
Arthur	Thomas	8	1794	35	juror
Arthur	Thomas	5	1796	58	plt
Arthur	Thomas	5	1796	58	def
Arthur	Thomas	2	1797	70	def
Ashley	Noah	7	1800	167	juror
Ashley	Noah	1	1801	177	juror
Ashmore	Hezakiah	7	1801	193	juror
Ashmore	Hezekiah		1792	14	def
Auld	Elizabeth	1	1802	197	victum
Auldman	Thomas	8	1795	48	juror
Austin	Archi	1	1801	178	juror
Avery	Waightstill	5	1794	25	plt
Ayers	Gentry	8	1797	87	juror
Bacon	Michael		1792	1	
Bacon	Michael		1792	21	juror
Bacon	Michael	2	1797	75	def
Bacon	Michael	8	1797	85	def
Baker	James	8	1796	64	juror
Baker	James	8	1796	65	juror
Baker	James	5	1797	77	juror
Baker	James	11	1797	96	juror
Baker	James	1	1798	106	plt
Baker	James	1	1798	109	juror

JEFFERSON COUNTY TENNESSEE COURT MINUTE BOOKS
INDEX 1783-1816

LAST	FIRST	MON	YEAR	PAGE	OTHER
Baker	James	1	1798	112	juror
Baker	James	7	1800	166	juror
Baker	John	2	1797	74	juror
Baker	John	4	1798	120	def
Baker	John	4	1799	141	def
Balch	John		1792	4	
Balch	John		1792	16	juror
Balch	John		1792	17	juror
Balch	John	11	1795	54	juror
Balch	John	5	1796	60	juror
Balch	William		1792	1	
Baldwin	Hute ?	1	1800	159	juror
Baldwin	Ute	1	1801	177	juror
Baldwin	Zenas	8	1794	30	juror
Banta	George		1792	1	
Barber	John	2	1793	110	juror
Barber	John	2	1795	42	juror
Barnhill	John	11	1797	94	plt
Barton	Isaac	1	1800	161	def
Barton	Isaac	7	1800	170	def
Bate	Roger		1792	9	juror
Bates	James	10	1798	131	def
Bates	James	7	1801	192	juror
Bates	John		1792	3	
Bates	John		1792	3	def
Bates	John		1792	9	juror
Bates	John		1792	11	juror
Bates	John	5	1795	45	def
Beach	Jesse	1	1802	196	juror
Beaver	Wm	5	1797	82	juror
Beaver	Wm	7	1799	141	juror
Beavers	Wm	2	1797	72	juror
Beavers	Wm	2	1797	74	juror
Beck	Daniel	8	1797	86	A & B
Beck	Daniel	1	1802	199	juror
Bedwell	Caleb	7	1799	157	juror
Bedwell	Caleb	1	1800	161	plt
Bedwell	Caleb	7	1800	170	plt
Beem	Jacob	8	1797	86	A & B

JEFFERSON COUNTY TENNESSEE COURT MINUTE BOOKS
INDEX 1783-1816

LAST	FIRST	MON	YEAR	PAGE	OTHER
Bell	Robert	8	1795	50	def
Bell	William		1792	3	
Bell	William		1792	7	juror
Bell	William		1792	22	plt
Bell	William		1792	23	juror
Bell	William	7	1798	121	plt
Bell	Wm	5	1794	29	juror
Bell	Wm	8	1794	30	juror
Bell	Wm	8	1797	85	juror
Bell	Wm	11	1797	93	juror
Bell	Wm	11	1797	94	juror
Berry	Robert	5	1796	57	juror
Berry	Robert	5	1796	58	juror
Berry	Robert	8	1796	63	juror
Berry	Robert	11	1796	66	juror
Berry	Robert	11	1796	69	juror
Berry	Robert	1	1798	109	juror
Berry	Robert	1	1798	115	juror
Berry	Robert	4	1799	139	juror
Berry	Robert	7	1802	206	juror
Bierd	Patrick	4	1801	180	juror
Biggam	Wm	8	1797	85	juror
Bird	Abraham	5	1796	59	juror
Bird	John	2	1797	70	juror
Bird	John	2	1797	71	juror
Bird	John	5	1797	78	juror
Bird	John	5	1797	80	juror
Bird	Thomas	5	1797	79	juror
Black	David		1792	4	plt
Black	David	8	1794	34	plt
Black	William		1792	17	plt
Black	William	8	1796	63	plt
Blackburn	Andrew	11	1796	68	juror
Blackburn	Andrew	1	1798	107	juror
Blackburn	William		1792	11	juror
Blair	Samuel		1792	20	juror
Blair	Samuel		1792	20	juror
Blankenship	James	8	1796	65	def
Blount	William		1792	3	plt

LAST	FIRST	MON	YEAR	PAGE	OTHER
Boggas	Bennett	5	1794	26	juror
Boggas	Bennett	8	1795	50	juror
Boggat	Bennett	5	1794	28	juror
Boid	Abraham	8	1795	49	juror
Bowan	James	5	1795	44	juror
Bowyer	Luke		1792	13	att.
Boyd	Wm	4	1799	138	juror
Bradford	Benjamin	4	1802	201	plt
Bradford	Benjamin	7	1802	207	plt
Bradford	Henry	5	1797	81	juror
Bradford	James	4	1802	203	jeff co.-sheriff
Bradford	John	4	1798	117	juror
Bradley	Lyon		1792	3	
Bradley	Lyon	5	1796	58	juror
Bradley	Sherrard		1792	9	juror
Bradley	Sherrard		1792	11	juror
Bradley	Sion		1792	7	juror
Bradley	Sion	5	1795	43	juror
Bradley	Sion	5	1796	57	juror
Bradley	William	11	1796	68	state ver.
Bradley	Wm	2	1797	72	juror
Bradshaw	James	7	1800	172	juror
Bradshaw	Wm	4	1801	182	juror
Branner	Michael	7	1801	187	juror
Branner	Michael	7	1802	206	juror
Brannum	Thomas	11	1797	100	plt
Brannum	Thomas	11	1797	102	plt
Brannum	Thomas	11	1797	102	plt
Brannum	Thomas	11	1797	103	plt
Brannum	Thomas	4	1798	117	plt
Brannum	Thomas	10	1798	126	plt
Brannum	Thomas	4	1799	139	plt
Brazelton	Isaac	11	1795	53	juror
Brazelton	Jacob		1792	3	
Brazelton	Jacob	8	1795	48	juror
Brazelton	Jacob	8	1795	48	juror
Brazelton	Jacob	5	1796	57	juror
Brazelton	Jacob	5	1796	58	juror
Brazelton	Jacob	5	1796	59	def

JEFFERSON COUNTY TENNESSEE COURT MINUTE BOOKS
INDEX 1783-1816

LAST	FIRST	MON	YEAR	PAGE	OTHER
Brazelton	John		1792	3	
Brazelton	John	11	1795	53	juror
Brazelton	Sam	8	1795	49	juror
Brazelton	William	5	1794	29	juror
Brazelton	William	4	1798	119	def
Brazelton	Wm	8	1794	30	juror
Brazelton	Wm	8	1794	31	juror
Brazelton	Wm	8	1794	32	juror
Brazelton	Wm	8	1794	33	juror
Brazelton	Wm	2	1795	41	juror
Brazelton	Wm	5	1796	57	juror
Brazelton	Wm	5	1796	58	juror
Brazelton	Wm	11	1796	68	juror
Brazelton	Wm	2	1797	70	juror
Brazelton	Wm	1	1798	107	juror
Brazelton	Wm	1	1798	108	juror
Brazelton	Wm	1	1798	110	juror
Brazelton	Wm	10	1798	127	juror
Brazelton	Wm	4	1800	163	juror
Brazelton	Wm	1	1801	176	juror
Brazelton	Wm	7	1801	187	juror
Brazelton	Wm Jr.	1	1798	110	juror
Brazelton	Wm Jr.	1	1798	111	juror
Brazelton	Wm Jr.	1	1798	112	juror
Brazelton	Wm Sr.	1	1798	110	juror
Brazelton	Wm Sr.	1	1798	111	juror
Brazelton	Wm Sr.	1	1798	112	juror
Brice	William	11	1795	56	def
Brickey	Peter	5	1797	78	juror
Brindle	Frazer	11	1797	100	def
Brindle	Frazer	11	1797	102	def
Brindle	Frazer	4	1798	117	def
Brindle	Frazer	4	1798	118	def
Brindle	George	11	1797	97	juror
Brindlee	George	11	1797	99	juror
Brindley	Frazer		1792	4	
Brindley	Frazer		1792	9	juror
Brindley	Frazer	10	1798	126	trespass
Brindley	Frazier	4	1799	139	def

JEFFERSON COUNTY TENNESSEE COURT MINUTE BOOKS
INDEX 1783-1816

LAST	FIRST	MON	YEAR	PAGE	OTHER
Brindley	George	5	1796	60	juror
Brindley	Richard		1792	15	juror
Brindley	Richard		1792	22	plt
Brindley	Stephen		1792	10	juror
Brinley	Richard		1792	4	
Brinley	Richard		1792	12	def
Britain	Wm	11	1797	99	juror
Britain	Wm	11	1797	101	juror
Brittain	Wm	11	1797	97	juror
Brittain	Wm	7	1798	122	juror
Brittain	Wm	10	1798	127	juror
Bronw	John	5	1794	29	juror
Bronw	John	8	1794	35	def
Brown	Alex	11	1795	53	juror
Brown	Claiborn		1792	11	affray
Brown	David		1792	7	juror
Brown	David		1792	9	juror
Brown	David		1792	11	juror
Brown	David		1792	12	juror
Brown	David		1792	13	juror
Brown	David		1792	14	juror
Brown	David		1792	16	juror
Brown	David		1792	17	juror
Brown	David	4	1799	135	juror
Brown	David	4	1799	140	plt
Brown	David	7	1799	141	juror
Brown	David	7	1799	156	juror
Brown	George	11	1797	103	def
Brown	George	4	1800	163	plt
Brown	John		1792	22	juror
Brown	John	5	1794	27	juror
Brown	John	8	1794	34	juror
Brown	Thomas	10	1798	130	def
Brown	Thomas	7	1799	156	def
Brown	Wm	5	1797	82	juror
Brown	Wm	8	1797	86	juror
Bryan	Andrew		1792	1	
Bryan	Thomas		1792	3	
Bryan	William		1792	22	juror

LAST	FIRST	MON	YEAR	PAGE	OTHER
Bryan	William		1792	23	juror
Bryan	William	5	1794	27	juror
Bryan	William	5	1794	28	def
Bryan	Wm		1792	21	juror
Bryan	Wm	2	1793	110	juror
Bryan	Wm	8	1794	35	juror
Bryan	Wm	11	1795	53	juror
Bryan	Wm	7	1798	123	juror
Buckingham	Wm	8	1794	34	juror
Buckner	Mary	8	1797	86	victum
Buckner	Mary	10	1798	127	larceny
Buckner	Patrick	1	1798	108	def
Bullar	John		1792	4	
Bullard	Christopher		1792	22	juror
Bullard	Isaac		1792	4	
Bullard	Isaac		1792	22	juror
Bullard	Isaac	5	1795	45	juror
Bullard	John		1792	22	juror
Bullard	John	11	1795	52	juror
Bullard	John	2	1797	74	juror
Bullard	Joseph Heirs	11	1795	54	def
Bullard	Joseph Heirs	2	1797	70	def
Burk	John		1792	12	juror
Burke	John	5	1796	60	juror
Burke	John	2	1797	72	juror
Burke	John	7	1799	152	def
Burke	John	7	1799	152	def
Burns	Isaac	7	1799	151	def
Burns	James	7	1799	151	def
Burris	Elijah	5	1795	45	juror
Burton	John	4	1801	182	def
Butler	John	2	1797	72	juror
Caldwell	Wm	5	1794	29	juror
Caldwell	Wm	8	1794	30	juror
Caldwell	Wm	8	1794	31	juror
Caldwell	Wm	8	1794	33	juror
Caldwell	Wm	5	1797	77	juror
Caldwell	Wm	7	1800	166	juror
Callahan	Charles	8	1795	48	juror

JEFFERSON COUNTY TENNESSEE COURT MINUTE BOOKS
INDEX 1783-1816

LAST	FIRST	MON	YEAR	PAGE	OTHER
Callahan	Charles	8	1795	48	juror
Callahan	Charles	8	1797	90	juror
Callahan	Thomas	10	1798	126	juror
Callister	Wm	1	1800	161	juror
Calllum	John	11	1795	53	juror
Callum	John	5	1796	61	plt
Campbell	Alex	2	1797	70	juror
Campbell	Alex	2	1797	71	juror
Campbell	Alex	8	1797	85	juror
Campbell	Alex	8	1797	88	juror
Campbell	Alex	11	1797	93	juror
Campbell	Alex	11	1797	94	juror
Campbell	Alex	11	1797	95	juror
Campbell	Alex	11	1797	99	juror
Campbell	Alex	11	1797	100	juror
Campbell	Alex	1	1798	110	juror
Campbell	Alex	1	1798	112	juror
Campbell	Alexander		1792	9	plt
Campbell	Alexander	1	1798	106	plt
Campbell	Alexander	1	1798	111	juror
Campbell	Andrew		1792	3	
Campbell	Andrew	4	1801	180	def
Campbell	David		1792	6	plt
Campbell	James	8	1796	64	juror
Campbell	James	8	1796	65	juror
Campbell	James	5	1797	78	juror
Campbell	James	5	1797	78	juror
Campbell	James	5	1797	79	juror
Campbell	James	5	1797	80	juror
Campbell	James	8	1797	85	juror
Campbell	James	8	1797	86	juror
Campbell	James	11	1797	95	juror
Campbell	James	11	1797	99	juror
Campbell	James	11	1797	100	juror
Campbell	James	11	1797	101	juror
Campbell	James	7	1798	124	juror
Campbell	John		1792	10	juror
Campbell	John		1792	14	juror
Campbell	John	8	1795	50	juror

JEFFERSON COUNTY TENNESSEE COURT MINUTE BOOKS
INDEX 1783-1816

LAST	FIRST	MON	YEAR	PAGE	OTHER
Campbell	John	4	1801	180	def
Campbell	John	7	1801	191	adm-def
Campbell	Joseph	7	1799	146	riot
Campbell	Sam	7	1799	155	juror
Campbell	William		1792	2	
Campbell	William		1792	13	juror
Campbell	William	5	1794	26	plt
Campbell	Wm	5	1794	25	juror
Campbell	Wm	5	1794	28	juror
Campbell	Wm	8	1794	33	juror
Campbell	Wm	8	1794	33	def
Campbell	Wm	11	1795	52	def
Campbell	Wm	5	1796	60	juror
Campbell	Wm	5	1796	62	juror
Campbell	Wm	8	1796	63	def
Campbell	Wm	8	1796	64	juror
Campbell	Wm	2	1797	70	juror
Campbell	Wm	2	1797	71	juror
Campbell	Wm	8	1797	85	juror
Cannnon	Zachariah	1	1801	177	juror
Cannon	James	1	1802	199	juror
Cannon	Thomas		1792	15	juror
Cannon	Thomas		1792	16	juror
Cannon	Thomas		1792	17	juror
Cannon	Thomas		1792	18	juror
Cannon	Thomas		1792	19	juror
Cannon	Thomas	5	1797	78	juror
Cannon	Thomas	5	1797	79	juror
Cannon	Thomas	5	1797	80	juror
Cannon	Thomas	1	1798	116	juror
Cannon	Zachariah	7	1800	172	juror
Canon	James	7	1799	141	juror
Canon	Sam	8	1794	34	juror
Canon	Sam	7	1800	172	juror
Canon	Thomas	4	1798	117	juror
Cappuck	Thomas	1	1798	112	juror
Carlock	Abraham		1792	8	juror
Carlock	Abraham		1792	11	juror
Carlock	Abraham	5	1794	26	def

LAST	FIRST	MON	YEAR	PAGE	OTHER
Carlock	Abraham	5	1796	58	plt
Carlock	Isaac		1792	21	juror
Carlock	Isaac	8	1796	63	juror
Carman	John	10	1798	127	juror
Carmichael	James	10	1800	175	plt
Carmichael	James	1	1801	176	plt
Carnes	Adam	1	1799	133	def
Carper	Jacob	5	1795	46	plt
Carrigor	Godfrey	5	1796	60	plt
Carron	John	8	1796	65	juror
Carson	Adam	11	1796	68	juror
Carson	Adam	1	1799	132	juror
Carson	Andrew		1792	17	juror
Carson	Andrew		1792	18	juror
Carson	David	5	1794	26	juror
Carson	David	11	1795	56	juror
Carson	David	4	1799	139	juror
Carson	John	5	1794	26	juror
Carson	John	2	1795	38	juror
Carson	John	11	1795	52	juror
Carson	John	11	1795	55	juror
Carson	John	2	1797	74	juror
Carson	John	4	1799	136	juror
Carson	Robert		1792	17	juror
Carson	Robert	2	1795	37	juror
Carson	Robert	1	1802	196	juror
Carson	Sam	5	1794	28	juror
Carson	Sam	1	1800	161	juror
Carson	Sam	1	1801	177	juror
Carson	Sam	4	1802	202	juror
Carson	Samuel		1792	19	juror
Carson	Samuel	5	1794	26	juror
Carter	Henry	4	1802	202	A & B
Carter	Samuel	4	1802	201	plt
Carver	William	11	1796	68	state ver.
Cash	John	11	1795	55	juror
Castle	George	4	1802	201	juror
Cate	John	7	1799	155	juror
Cate	Thomas	1	1801	178	juror

JEFFERSON COUNTY TENNESSEE COURT MINUTE BOOKS
INDEX 1783-1816

LAST	FIRST	MON	YEAR	PAGE	OTHER
Cate	Wm	11	1796	68	juror
Chamberlain	Ninian	5	1797	81	plt
Cheek	Jesse	10	1798	130	plt
Cheek	Jesse	7	1799	155	plt
Cheek	Jesse	7	1799	156	plt
Cheek	Jesse	7	1802	206	juror
Cheek	William		1792	12	juror
Cheek	William		1792	17	juror
Cheek	William		1792	18	juror
Cheek	William	4	1802	202	juror
Chilton	James	11	1797	100	juror
Chilton	Thomas	2	1797	74	def
Christian	Thomas		1792	9	juror
Christian	Thomas	5	1796	57	juror
Christian	Thomas	5	1796	62	juror
Christian	Thomas	8	1796	63	juror
Churchman	Edward	4	1799	138	juror
Clack	John	5	194	27	juror
Clack	John		1792	21	juror
Clack	John	5	1794	29	juror
Clark	Ensley	5	1797	82	juror
Clark	John	11	1795	56	plt
Clark	Wm	5	1797	77	juror
Cline	Carper	1	1799	134	def
Clingan	Edward	8	1795	50	juror
Clingan	Edward	11	1795	53	juror
Clingan	Thomas	2	1795	41	def
Clingan	Thomas	5	1796	62	def
Clingar	Edward	2	1795	38	juror
Cobb	Etheldred		1792	10	larceny
Cobb	Etheldred	5	1794	25	def
Cobb	Wm	1	1798	115	plt
Cochran	Job	5	1796	62	juror
Cochran	Job	8	1796	63	juror
Cochran	Job	2	1797	72	T.A.B
Coffee	Robert	4	1800	164	juror
Coffman	Isaac	2	1797	74	juror
Coffman	James	1	1800	159	juror
Cofman	Andrew		1792	22	juror

JEFFERSON COUNTY TENNESSEE COURT MINUTE BOOKS
INDEX 1783-1816

LAST	FIRST	MON	YEAR	PAGE	OTHER
Cofman	Andrew	5	1794	26	juror
Cofman	Andrew	8	1794	33	plt
Cofman	Andrew	2	1797	74	plt
Cofman	Isaac	5	1794	26	juror
Cofman	Isaac	5	1794	26	juror
Collingsworth	John		1792	13	juror
Collins	John		1792	12	juror
Collins	Richard	10	1800	174	larceny
Collins	Richard	4	1801	184	larceny
Collinsworth	Coventor		1792	23	juror
Collinsworth	Coverton	5	1796	59	juror
Collinsworth	John		1792	14	juror
Collinsworth	John	5	1796	59	juror
Collinsworth	John	4	1799	140	def
Collinsworth	John	7	1799	153	def
Colter	John	5	1797	83	larceny
Congleton	Moses	5	1794	28	def
Congleton	Robert	5	1794	28	def
Conway	William	7	1799	152	plt
Coons	John	2	1795	38	juror
Coons	Michael	1	1800	161	juror
Coons	Michael	1	1801	179	plt
Coons	Michael	4	1801	183	juror
Coons	Michale	1	1801	178	juror
Coons	Rebecca	7	1799	158	victum
Coontz	John	5	1795	46	juror
Coontz	John	11	1795	54	juror
Cooper	Wm	11	1797	99	juror
Cooper	Wm	11	1797	100	juror
Cope	John	5	1797	77	juror
Cope	John	5	1797	78	juror
Cope	Stephen		1792	13	juror
Copeland	Rickets	4	1800	164	prosecuter
Copeland	Stephen	8	1794	31	juror
Copeland	Zacheus	7	1801	187	juror
Coppuck	Isaiah	4	1801	183	juror
Coppuck	Joseph	7	1800	166	juror
Coppuck	Joseph	4	1801	182	juror
Coppuck	Joseph	7	1801	193	juror

JEFFERSON COUNTY TENNESSEE COURT MINUTE BOOKS
INDEX 1783-1816

LAST	FIRST	MON	YEAR	PAGE	OTHER
Coppuck	Thomas	1	1798	113	juror
Corbet	John	1	1798	106	juror
Corbett	Ellizabeth	7	1800	171	def
Corbit	John	11	1797	97	juror
Corbit	John	1	1798	107	juror
Corbit	John	1	1798	108	juror
Corbit	John	1	1798	111	def
Corbit	John	1	1798	111	juror
Corman	John	1	1801	176	juror
Corron	John	8	1796	64	juror
Costalous	Edward	7	1799	142	juror
Coteney	John	4	1802	204	plt
Cottinger	Wm	8	1797	85	juror
Cottingham	Elisha	1	1798	112	juror
Cottingham	Elisha	1	1798	113	juror
Countz	John	8	1795	50	juror
Countz	John	8	1795	51	juror
Countz	John	11	1795	56	juror
Countz	John	5	1796	57	juror
Countz	Michael	2	1793	110	juror
Cowan	Andrew	5	1796	57	juror
Cowan	Andrew	8	1797	90	juror
Cowan	James	2	1797	75	juror
Cowan	James	1	1798	115	juror
Cowan	James	7	1799	149	juror
Cowan	James	7	1799	150	plt
Cowan	John		1792	4	
Cowan	John		1792	23	juror
Cowan	John	8	1796	63	juror
Cowan	John	4	1801	182	juror
Cowan	John	7	1801	187	juror
Cowan	John	7	1801	189	def
Cowan	Robert	5	1794	26	juror
Cowan	Robert	5	1795	44	juror
Cowan	Robert	8	1795	51	juror
Cowan	Robert	5	1797	84	juror
Cowan	Robert	1	1799	132	juror
Cowan	Robert	1	1799	134	def
Cowan	Robert	4	1799	136	juror

JEFFERSON COUNTY TENNESSEE COURT MINUTE BOOKS
INDEX 1783-1816

LAST	FIRST	MON	YEAR	PAGE	OTHER
Cowan	Sam	5	1795	44	juror
Cowan	Sam	1	1799	132	juror
Cowan	Sam	7	1799	156	juror
Cowan	Sam	1	1801	178	juror
Cower	James	5	1795	45	juror
Cox	Edward	1	1798	110	plt
Cox	Harman	4	1801	181	witness
Cox	Henry	8	1795	49	juror
Cox	Henry	8	1795	50	def
Cox	Joab	4	1799	136	juror
Cox	Joab	7	1799	157	juror
Cox	John	11	1797	93	juror
Cox	John	11	1797	94	juror
Cox	Solomon	4	1799	136	juror
Cox	William	7	1798	125	plt
Cox	Wm	7	1800	167	juror
Cristian	James	5	1795	43	juror
Crockett	John	8	1797	88	juror
Crockett	John	8	1797	90	juror
Crockett	John & Dewey	11	1795	52	plt
Cross	William	7	1801	187	plt
Cross	William	1	1802	196	plt
Cuningham	James	2	1795	38	juror
Cuningham	James	2	1795	41	juror
Cunningham	Matthew	5	1797	78	juror
Dairs	Brittain	1	1800	160	plt
Damerall	Joseph	1	1798	115	juror
Dameron	Jos	8	1797	89	juror
Dameron	Joseph	11	1795	52	juror
Dameron	Joseph	11	1795	52	juror
Dameron	Joseph	11	1795	53	juror
Dameron	Joseph	5	1796	62	juror
Dameron	Joseph	7	1800	166	plt
Dameron	Joseph	10	1800	173	plt
Dameron	Joseph	7	1801	192	juror
Dameron	Jospeh	7	1799	156	juror
Damrell	Joseph	11	1797	101	plt
Daniel	John	5	1796	60	juror
Daniel	John	4	1802	202	victum

JEFFERSON COUNTY TENNESSEE COURT MINUTE BOOKS
INDEX 1783-1816

LAST	FIRST	MON	YEAR	PAGE	OTHER
Davia	James	1	1801	178	juror
Davidson	Wm	8	1797	85	plt
Davis	Arthur		1792	11	juror
Davis	Arthur	7	1799	151	juror
Davis	Ben	5	1795	46	juror
Davis	Benjamin	11	1797	94	plt
Davis	Benjamin	11	1797	101	def
Davis	Bozdell	8	1797	90	juror
Davis	Elizabeth	11	1797	105	adm-plt
Davis	Elizabeth	1	1799	132	plt
Davis	Fanny	8	1797	90	victum
Davis	James	1	1798	116	juror
Davis	James	4	1799	138	juror
Davis	James	7	1800	168	misdemeanor
Davis	James	7	1800	172	juror
Davis	James	1	1802	199	juror
Davis	James	4	1802	201	juror
Davis	Nicholas		1792	4	
Davis	Nicholas		1792	6	juror
Davis	Nicholas	8	1794	30	juror
Davis	Nicholas	8	1797	89	juror
Davis	Nicholas	7	1798	121	juror
Davis	Nicholas	7	1801	193	juror
Davis	Thomas	11	1797	99	juror
Davis	Thomas	11	1797	100	juror
Davis	Wm	4	1799	138	juror
Davison	Elizabeth	11	1797	102	plt
Day	Jesse	4	1801	182	juror
Day	John	4	1800	163	def
Day	John	4	1801	182	juror
Day	John	4	1801	186	def
Dean	Francis	8	1795	51	juror
Dean	Francis	11	1795	52	juror
Dean	Francis	11	1795	53	juror
Dean	John		1792	23	juror
Dean	John	5	1794	26	juror
Dean	John	5	1794	27	juror
Dean	John	5	1794	29	juror
Dean	John	8	1795	49	juror

JEFFERSON COUNTY TENNESSEE COURT MINUTE BOOKS
INDEX 1783-1816

LAST	FIRST	MON	YEAR	PAGE	OTHER
Dean	John	8	1795	51	juror
Dean	John	11	1795	52	juror
Dean	John	11	1795	53	juror
Dean	John	8	1796	63	juror
Dean	John	8	1796	64	juror
Dean	John	8	1796	64	juror
Dean	John	2	1797	74	juror
Dean	Robert	8	1795	48	juror
Dean	Robert	11	1795	56	juror
Dennison	John	5	1796	57	juror
Dennison	John	5	1796	58	juror
Denton	Jacob	4	1800	164	witness
Denton	John		1792	1	
Denton	John	2	1797	70	juror
Denton	John	2	1797	71	juror
Denton	Joseph	11	1797	95	plt
Denton	Thomas		1792	18	juror
Denton	Thomas	2	1795	36	def
Denton	Thomas	2	1795	37	juror
Denton	Thomas	11	1795	56	def
Dinwoody	Samuel	7	1800	171	plt
Dobkin	Jacob		1792	3	plt
Dobkin	Reuben	7	1799	141	juror
Dobkin	Reuben	7	1801	192	def
Docker	Thomas	4	1802	201	juror
Doggett	Jacob		1792	21	def
Doggett	Jacob	2	1793	110	juror
Doggett	Jacob	2	1793	110	def
Doggett	John	2	1793	110	juror
Doggett	Miller	5	1797	81	juror
Doggett	Miller	5	1797	82	juror
Doggett	Miller	10	1798	126	juror
Doggett	Milller	5	1797	78	juror
Doherty	George	5	1795	45	plt
Doherty	George	7	1801	189	plt
Doherty	James		1792	23	juror
Doherty	James	2	1797	75	juror
Doherty	James	1	1801	176	def
Doherty	James	7	1801	192	plt

LAST	FIRST	MON	YEAR	PAGE	OTHER
Doherty	Joseph		1792	3	
Doherty	Wm	8	1795	49	juror
Donalson	Andrew		1792	15	juror
Donalson	Andrew		1792	17	juror
Donalson	Andrew		1792	18	juror
Donelson	Stokely	7	1799	156	def
Donelson	Stokely	1	1801	176	def
Donelson	Thomas	7	1799	142	def
Donelson	W.		1792	16	juror
Donelson	William	5	1794	27	plt
Dougherty	James		1792	4	
Doughty	Ben	8	1797	87	juror
Douglas	Jonathan	2	1795	42	def
Douglass	Robert		1792	18	juror
Douglass	Robert		1792	22	juror
Douglass	Robert	8	1794	30	plt
Douglass	Robert	2	1795	36	juror
Douglass	Robert	2	1795	37	juror
Douglass	Robert	2	1795	38	plt
Drenaway	Elijah	5	1797	78	juror
Dreneway	Elijah	5	1797	79	juror
Dreneway	Elijah	5	1797	80	juror
Dreneway	Elijah	8	1797	86	juror
Drenneway	Elijah	8	1797	91	def
Duncan	Craven	8	1797	90	juror
Durgen	John	1	1798	114	def
Durofrett	Daniel	5	1795	45	juror
Durossett	Daniel	4	1798	117	juror
Durossett	Daniel	7	1799	141	juror
Durossett	Sam	8	1795	48	juror
Durossett	Sam	8	1795	48	juror
Durossett	Sam	8	1795	49	juror
Durossett	Sam	8	1795	51	juror
Durossett	Sam	5	1796	60	juror
Durossett	Sam	11	1796	69	juror
Durossett	Sam	8	1797	85	def
Durossett	Samuel	2	1797	75	def
Durossett	Samuel	7	1799	155	plt
Durossett	Samuel	1	1800	159	plt

JEFFERSON COUNTY TENNESSEE COURT MINUTE BOOKS
INDEX 1783-1816

LAST	FIRST	MON	YEAR	PAGE	OTHER
Dyer	Thomas	10	1800	175	def
Dyer	Thomas	1	1801	176	def
Earls	Thomas	2	1797	70	juror
Earls	Thomas	2	1797	71	juror
Earls	Thomas	11	1797	102	def
Edgar	Alex	4	1799	136	juror
Edgar	Andrew	8	1794	30	juror
Edgar	Andrew	8	1795	50	juror
Edgar	Andrew	5	1796	57	juror
Edgar	Andrew	1	1798	116	juror
Edgar	Andrew	110	1798	127	juror
Edgar	Andrew	4	1799	139	juror
Edgar	Andrew	1	1800	159	juror
Edgar	George		1792	3	
Edgar	George	5	1795	45	plt
Edgar	George	5	1796	57	juror
Edgar	George	5	1796	58	juror
Edmunds	John	7	1801	192	juror
Edwards	Evan		1792	4	def
Eldridge	Simeon	4	1799	138	juror
Eldridge	Simeon	7	1799	149	juror
Eldridge	Simeon	7	1799	151	plt
Eller	James	1	1798	111	juror
Elliot	James		1792	12	juror
Elliot	James	5	1796	61	def
Elliot	William		1792	5	juror
Elliot	William		1792	6	juror
Elliot	Wm	11	1797	97	juror
Elliott	James	11	1795	53	juror
Elliott	James	7	1801	192	juror
Elliott	Wm	4	1801	182	juror
Ellis	Chirstopher	8	1796	64	def
Ellis	James	1	1798	112	juror
Ellis	James	1	1798	116	juror
Ellis	James	4	1798	117	juror
Ellis	James	4	1798	119	plt
Ellis	James	10	1798	126	juror
Ellis	James	4	1799	135	juror
Ellis	James	4	1799	136	plt

LAST	FIRST	MON	YEAR	PAGE	OTHER
Ellis	James	4	1799	136	def
Ellis	James	7	1799	153	juror
Ellis	James	1	1801	176	juror
Ellis	James	4	1801	181	witness
Ellis	Joseph	10	1798	126	juror
Ellis	Lewis	4	1798	117	juror
Ellis	Lewis	10	1798	126	juror
Ellis	Lewis	7	1799	149	juror
Ellis	Lewis	1	1801	178	juror
Ellis	Lewis	4	1802	201	juror
Ellis	Nehemiah	8	1794	30	juror
Ellis	William		1792	4	
Elmore	Joel	5	1796	58	juror
Elmore	Joel	8	1796	63	juror
Elmore	Joel	8	1796	63	juror
Elmore	Joel	8	1797	85	juror
Erwin	Sam	8	1794	33	juror
Erwin	Sam	8	1794	34	juror
Erwin	Sam	8	1794	35	juror
Erwin	Sam	2	1795	41	juror
Evans	Andrew	5	1795	46	def
Evans	George	7	1801	193	def
Evans	Jacob	5	1795	44	juror
Evans	Jacob	5	1796	57	juror
Evans	John		1792	4	
Evans	John	2	1797	70	juror
Evans	Wm	5	1796	61	plt
Ewing	Robert	5	1794	26	juror
Ewing	Robert	5	1794	27	juror
Ewing	Robert	5	1794	29	juror
Ewing	Susanah	8	1794	31	victum
Fellers	John	4	1802	202	juror
Ferril	James		1792	14	juror
Ferril	James	5	1795	44	juror
Ferril	James	5	1795	44	juror
Ferrill	James	8	1794	34	juror
Fields	Obediah	4	1799	141	plt
Fincher	Isaac	5	1794	26	juror
Fine	Peter	11	1795	53	juror

JEFFERSON COUNTY TENNESSEE COURT MINUTE BOOKS
INDEX 1783-1816

LAST	FIRST	MON	YEAR	PAGE	OTHER
Fine	Peter	11	1795	54	juror
Fine	Peter	5	1796	60	juror
Fine	Peter	5	1796	61	plt
Fippen	Thomas	2	1795	38	juror
Fitchgerald	Garrett	8	1794	33	def
Fitzgerald	Garret	11	1797	99	def
Fitzgerald	Garrett	5	1797	80	def
Fitzgerald	Garrett	1	1801	178	plt
Flippen	Thomas		1792	15	juror
Flippen	Thomas		1792	16	juror
Flippen	Thomas	5	1795	43	juror
Fomalt	John	7	1802	206	plt
Forbish	Samuel	4	1802	201	juror
Forbish	Thomas	4	1802	201	juror
Ford	Ben	5	1794	27	juror
Ford	Ben	5	1794	29	juror
Ford	Ben	8	1794	34	juror
Ford	Ben	8	1794	35	juror
Ford	Ben	2	1795	38	juror
Ford	Ben	2	1795	41	juror
Ford	Ben	11	1795	53	juror
Ford	Ben	8	1797	86	juror
Ford	Ben	8	1797	91	plt
Ford	Ben	11	1797	94	def
Ford	Ben	7	1799	151	juror
Ford	Ben	1	1800	161	def
Ford	Benjamin		1792	14	juror
Ford	Benjamin		1792	15	juror
Ford	Benjamin	2	1797	71	T.A.B.
Ford	Benjamin	7	1799	154	def
Ford	John	7	1800	167	juror
Ford	Mortica	8	1795	51	plt
Ford	Mortica	11	1795	54	plt
Formalt	John	4	1801	182	juror
Formalt	John	7	1801	187	juror
Formalt	John	4	1802	200	def
Formsalt	John	1	1802	196	juror
Formwalt	John	7	1801	189	victum
Formwalt	John Jr.	7	1801	189	witness

JEFFERSON COUNTY TENNESSEE COURT MINUTE BOOKS
INDEX 1783-1816

LAST	FIRST	MON	YEAR	PAGE	OTHER
Foute	Jacob	7	1801	187	juror
Fowler	Jacob	7	1800	166	def
Fowler	Jacob	1	1801	179	def
Fowler	Thomas	2	1797	74	juror
Fox	Abraham	5	1795	45	juror
Frame	David		1792	3	
Frame	David	8	1794	31	juror
Frazer	Hugh	5	1795	47	victum
Fryar	John	2	1795	37	juror
Fryar	John	2	1795	38	def
Fryar	John	5	1795	43	juror
Fryar	John	8	1795	50	juror
Fryar	John	8	1795	51	juror
Fryar	John	5	1796	58	def
Galbreith	John	5	1795	44	plt
Gamble	Robert	4	1801	180	plt
Gamble	Robert	4	1801	180	plt
Garrett	Thomas	11	1795	53	juror
Garrett	Thomas	11	1795	55	juror
Garrett	Thomas	5	1796	60	juror
Garrett	Wm	1	1800	161	juror
Gass	Sam	8	1797	89	juror
Gass	Sam	1	1798	111	juror
Gentry	Bartlett	11	1795	54	juror
Gentry	Bartlett	1	1798	106	juror
Gentry	Bartlett	1	1798	107	juror
Gentry	Bartlett	1	1798	108	juror
Gentry	Bartlett	1	1798	110	juror
Gentry	Bartlett	4	1802	200	juror
Gentry	Martin	4	1799	136	juror
Gentry	Martin	7	1800	166	juror
Gentry	Robert		1792	24	juror
Gentry	Robert	10	1798	127	juror
George	Edward		1792	20	juror
George	Edward		1792	20	juror
George	Edward		1792	24	juror
George	Edward	11	1795	56	juror
George	Edward	1	1801	177	juror
George	Samuel	1	1799	132	plt

JEFFERSON COUNTY TENNESSEE COURT MINUTE BOOKS
INDEX 1783-1816

LAST	FIRST	MON	YEAR	PAGE	OTHER
George	Silas	4	1801	183	juror
Gibson	John	8	1794	30	juror
Gibson	John	2	1795	38	juror
Gibson	John	5	1795	43	juror
Gibson	Wm	5	1797	82	juror
Gibson	Wm	8	1797	87	assault
Gilbert	Felix	5	1796	59	juror
Gilbert	Felix	8	1796	64	juror
Gilbert	Felix	8	1797	88	juror
Gilbert	John	8	1796	64	juror
Gilbreath	Thomas	1	1801	176	juror
Gilbreath	Thomas	1	1801	177	juror
Gilbreath	Thomas	7	1801	193	juror
Gilliland	John		1792	1	
Gilliland	John		1792	22	def
Gilliland	John	5	1794	28	juror
Gilliland	John	5	1796	61	exr-def
Gilliland	John	2	1797	71	exr-def
Gilliland	John	5	1797	79	exr-def
Gilliland	John	11	1797	99	juror
Gilliland	John	11	1797	100	juror
Gilliland	Robert	5	1795	44	juror
Gilliland	Robert	8	1795	48	juror
Gilliland	Robert	8	1795	48	juror
Gilliland	Robert	11	1795	55	juror
Gist	Joshua		1792	10	juror
Gist	Sam	8	1795	50	juror
Gist	Sam	7	1801	193	juror
Gist	Samuel	8	1794	30	juror
Gist	Wm	8	1795	49	juror
Gist	Wm	11	1795	52	juror
Givens	Patrick	7	1799	155	juror
Glass	John	7	1800	166	juror
Glass	John	4	1801	182	juror
Glass	John	7	1801	187	juror
Glass	John	7	1801	191	plt
Goforth	William		1792	5	juror
Goforth	William		1792	6	juror
Going	Anne	7	1801	189	witness

JEFFERSON COUNTY TENNESSEE COURT MINUTE BOOKS
INDEX 1783-1816

LAST	FIRST	MON	YEAR	PAGE	OTHER
Going	Daniel	4	1801	180	juror
Going	Daniel	4	1801	182	juror
Gordon	George		1792	23	juror
Gordon	George	11	1795	54	juror
Gordon	George	11	1797	103	plt
Gordon	George	11	1797	105	plt
Gordon	George	10	1798	130	plt
Gordon	George	4	1800	164	plt
Gordon	George	7	1801	188	larceny
Gordon	Robert	10	1798	128	def
Gordon	Robert	1	1800	159	juror
Gore	Ambrose	7	1798	121	juror
Gore	Ambrose	7	1798	122	juror
Gore	Ambrose	7	1798	125	plt
Gore	Ambrose	4	1799	139	juror
Gore	John	1	1798	111	def
Gore	John	1	1798	112	def
Grace	Richard	1	1798	113	juror
Grace	Richard	7	1799	155	juror
Grace ?	Richard	1	1798	112	juror
Graham	George		1792	3	
Graham	George		1792	21	juror
Graham	George	8	1795	49	juror
Graham	George	1	1799	133	def
Graham	George	7	1801	191	def
Graham	George	7	1802	207	def
Gray	Thomas	4	1800	163	plt
Gray	Wm	8	1794	33	juror
Gray	Wm	8	1794	35	juror
Gray	Wm	2	1795	41	juror
Gray	Wm	8	1795	50	plt
Green	Francis	4	1799	137	A & B
Green	Francis	4	1799	138	A & B
Green	John	5	1797	84	juror
Green	John	7	1801	191	plt
Greene	George	5	1797	78	def
Greene	John		1792	20	juror
Greene	John		1792	20	juror
Greene	John	11	1797	97	juror

LAST	FIRST	MON	YEAR	PAGE	OTHER
Greene	John	11	1797	101	juror
Greene	John	1	1798	110	juror
Greene	John	1	1798	111	juror
Greene	John	1	1798	112	juror
Greene	John	4	1798	118	plt
Greene	John	7	1798	124	juror
Greene	John	4	1801	183	plt
Greene	John	7	1801	187	plt
Greene	John	7	1802	207	def
Greene	Polly	1	1802	197	A & B
Greer	Thomas	8	1797	93	plt
Greer	Thomas	7	1798	123	juror
Grier	David	5	1795	44	plt
Grier	Dunlop &	8	1794	35	plt
Grier	James	11	1797	93	juror
Grier	James	11	1797	94	juror
Grier	James	11	1797	99	juror
Grier	Thomas	11	1797	99	juror
Grier	Thomas	11	1797	100	juror
Grier	Thomas	1	1798	107	juror
Grier	Thomas	1	1798	114	plt
Grier	Thomas	1	1798	115	juror
Grier	Thomas	1	1798	116	juror
Grier	Thomas	10	1798	130	plt
Grier	Thomas	1	1799	134	plt
Grier	Thomas	7	1799	149	juror
Grier	Thomas	7	1799	153	juror
Griffe	Thomas		1792	18	juror
Griffin	Caleb	5	1797	78	juror
Griffin	Caleb	5	1797	80	juror
Griffin	Caleb	1	1798	112	juror
Griffin	Caleb	7	1799	157	juror
Griffin	Joseph M. & Son	7	1802	207	plt
Griffin	Spencer	7	1801	193	juror
Griffin	Spencer	1	1802	199	juror
Griffin	Thomas		1792	17	juror
Grindstaff	Jacob	8	1794	34	juror
Grindstaff	Jacob	2	1795	36	juror
Grindstaff	Jacob	2	1795	37	juror

JEFFERSON COUNTY TENNESSEE COURT MINUTE BOOKS
INDEX 1783-1816

LAST	FIRST	MON	YEAR	PAGE	OTHER
Grindstaff	Jacob	8	1797	90	A & B
Grisham	Robert	4	1799	136	juror
Grisham	Robert	7	1799	157	juror
Grisham	Thomas	1	1798	110	juror
Grisham	Thompson	1	1798	110	juror
Grisham	Thompson	1	1798	111	plt
Grisham	Thompson	1	1798	113	juror
Grisham	Thompson	1	1798	116	juror
Grisham	Thompson	7	1799	149	juror
Grisham	Thompson	4	1801	180	juror
Haggard	Henry	4	1801	180	juror
Hail	Jonathan	2	1795	38	juror
Hainey	Spencer	5	1795	44	juror
Hall	Sarah	8	1794	31	robery
Hamil	John	4	1799	139	juror
Hamil	John	7	1801	187	juror
Hamilton	Francis	2	1795	36	A & B-rob
Hamilton	J.	10	1800	174	clerk
Hamilton	John		1792	23	juror
Hamilton	Joseph		1792	20	def
Hamilton	Joseph	5	1796	61	def
Hamilton	Joseph	8	1796	64	plt
Hamilton	Joseph	2	1797	71	exr-def
Hamilton	Joseph	5	1797	79	exr-def
Hammond	Thomas	7	1800	172	juror
Hammond	Thomas	1	1801	177	juror
Hampton	Edward	4	1799	139	juror
Hanbaugh	Jacob	4	1802	201	juror
Hanbough	Jacob		1792	17	juror
Hanbough	Jacob		1792	18	juror
Hanes	Christopher	2	1797	75	juror
Hanes	Christopher	1	1798	113	def
Hanes	John	8	1795	49	juror
Haney	Samuel		1792	10	juror
Haney	Spencer	5	1795	46	juror
Hannah	John	8	1796	64	plt
Hansil	Robert	7	1800	166	juror
Harbert	David	5	1796	61	def
Hardin	John		1792	6	plt

JEFFERSON COUNTY TENNESSEE COURT MINUTE BOOKS
INDEX 1783-1816

LAST	FIRST	MON	YEAR	PAGE	OTHER
Hardin	John	2	1793	110	juror
Hardin	John	2	1795	42	juror
Hardin	John	1	1798	106	def
Hargrove	Ben	5	1795	45	juror
Hargrove	Ben	8	1797	86	juror
Hargrove	Ben	8	1797	88	juror
Hargrove	Ben	11	1797	93	juror
Hargrove	Ben	11	1797	99	juror
Hargrove	Ben	11	1797	101	juror
Hargrove	Ben	1	1798	115	juror
Hargrove	Ben	4	1798	117	juror
Hargrove	Benjamin		1792	2	
Hargrove	Benjamin	8	1795	50	plt
Hargrove	Benjamin	8	1795	51	def
Hargrove	Benjamin	11	1796	65	plt
Hargrove	Eli	11	1796	67	w/Marshman
Hargrove	Joseph	11	1797	95	juror
Hargrove	Joseph	7	1799	155	juror
Harman	Jacob	11	1797	96	juror
Harman	Jacob	11	1797	99	juror
Harman	Levi ?	8	1797	86	juror
Harman	Lewis	11	1797	96	juror
Harman	Lewis	7	1801	187	juror
Harris	Isham		1792	1	
Harris	Isham		1792	21	juror
Harris	Isham	8	1797	92	plt
Harris	Sam		1792	6	juror
Harrison	Ben	8	1794	34	juror
Harrison	James		1792	4	
Harrison	James	5	1796	62	juror
Harrison	John	11	1797	101	juror
Harrison	John	4	1801	183	plt
Harvey	John	4	1798	120	plt
Harvey	John	7	1800	172	juror
Haskill/Haskal	John	5	1797	82	assault
Hasten	Daniel	8	1797	90	juror
Hasten	Daniel	11	1797	93	juror
Hastin	Daniel	11	1797	94	juror
Hastin	Daniel	11	1797	95	juror

LAST	FIRST	MON	YEAR	PAGE	OTHER
Hastins	Daniel	8	1797	85	juror
Hatler	Michael	7	1799	157	plt
Hatler	Michael	7	1800	167	juror
Hatler	Phillip	5	1795	43	def
Hatler	Phillip	8	1795	48	def
Havens	James	1	1798	106	juror
Havens	James	1	1798	107	juror
Havens	James	1	1798	108	juror
Havens	James	4	1802	200	juror
Haynes	John	1	1798	115	juror
Haynes	John	1	1798	116	juror
Hays	John	11	1797	99	juror
Hays	John	11	1797	100	juror
Hays	John	7	1801	193	juror
Hays	John	7	1802	206	juror
Hays	John	7	1802	208	witness
Hays	Sam	8	1795	49	juror
Hays	Sam	1	1798	107	juror
Hays	Sam	1	1798	109	juror
Hays	Sam	7	1798	122	juror
Hays	Sam	7	1799	141	juror
Hays	Sam	7	1799	156	juror
Hays	Sam	4	1801	182	juror
Hays	Sam	7	1801	187	def
Hays	William		1792	5	plt
Heavens	James	7	1799	141	juror
Hendeman	William		1792	8	def
Henderson	Dan	11	1795	53	juror
Henderson	Daniel	5	1794	25	juror
Henderson	Daniel	5	1797	79	juror
Henderson	Daniel	5	1797	79	juror
Henderson	Daniel	5	1797	80	juror
Henderson	Daniel	7	1798	123	juror
Henderson	Daniel	7	1798	124	juror
Henderson	David	2	1797	75	juror
Henderson	George	4	1798	117	juror
Henderson	George	7	1798	123	juror
Henderson	George	7	1799	156	juror
Henderson	James	10	1798	131	plt

JEFFERSON COUNTY TENNESSEE COURT MINUTE BOOKS
INDEX 1783-1816

LAST	FIRST	MON	YEAR	PAGE	OTHER
Henderson	James	1	1801	177	plt
Henderson	John		1792	3	
Henderson	John		1792	13	juror
Henderson	John		1792	16	juror
Henderson	John		1792	17	juror
Henderson	John		1792	24	juror
Henderson	John	8	1795	50	juror
Henderson	John	11	1795	54	juror
Henderson	John	8	1796	65	juror
Henderson	John	2	1797	74	juror
Henderson	John	5	1797	84	juror
Henderson	John	11	1797	94	juror
Henderson	John	1	1798	110	juror
Henderson	John	1	1799	132	juror
Henderson	John	7	1800	167	juror
Henderson	Sam	2	1795	38	juror
Henderson	Sam	5	1795	46	juror
Henderson	Sam	11	1795	55	juror
Henderson	Sam	11	1795	56	juror
Henderson	Sam	11	1796	68	juror
Henderson	Sam	2	1797	74	juror
Henderson	Sam	11	1797	95	def
Henderson	Sam	10	1798	127	juror
Henderson	Samuel	10	1798	131	plt
Henderson	Samuel	1	1799	132	def
Henderson	Samuel	7	1799	148	riot
Henderson	Thomas	5	1795	46	juror
Henderson	Thomas	11	1796	68	state ver.
Hendingale	Martin	5	1796	57	juror
Henry	Ezekiel		1792	5	juror
Henry	Ezekiel		1792	6	juror
Henry	Ezekiel	5	1794	27	juror
Henry	John		1792	10	juror
Henry	John		1792	16	juror
Henry	John		1792	19	juror
Henry	John	5	1794	28	juror
Henry	John	8	1794	34	juror
Henry	John	8	1794	35	juror
Henry	John	2	1795	36	juror

JEFFERSON COUNTY TENNESSEE COURT MINUTE BOOKS
INDEX 1783-1816

LAST	FIRST	MON	YEAR	PAGE	OTHER
Henry	William		1792	19	juror
Henry	Wm	8	1797	85	juror
Henry	Wm	7	1800	166	juror
Hester	Ferril	8	1795	49	juror
Heybard	John	4	1798	117	juror
Hibbard	Samuel		1792	16	plt
Hibbert	Jedediah	7	1799	155	juror
Hickle	George	1	1798	115	juror
Hickman	Ben	4	1800	163	juror
Hickman	Francis	7	1799	157	juror
Hickman	Francis	1	1801	176	plt
Higgins	John	1	1799	132	def
Hile	James	11	1797	93	juror
Hill	Abraham		1792	2	
Hill	Abraham	5	1796	59	juror
Hill	Abraham	5	1796	60	juror
Hill	Abraham	5	1796	62	juror
Hill	Abraham	8	1796	63	juror
Hill	Charles	5	1794	26	juror
Hill	Charles	8	1795	50	juror
Hill	Daniel		1792	3	
Hill	Daniel		1792	4	def
Hill	Daniel		1792	4	
Hill	Daniel		1792	6	juror
Hill	Daniel		1792	9	juror
Hill	Daniel		1792	13	juror
Hill	Daniel		1792	14	def
Hill	Daniel	11	1795	55	juror
Hill	Daniel	11	1796	69	juror
Hill	Daniel	1	1800	159	juror
Hill	Daniel	1	1800	160	def
Hill	Daniel	1	1800	161	juror
Hill	Daniel	7	1800	167	def
Hill	Daniel	4	1802	202	juror
Hill	James		1792	7	juror
Hill	James		1792	8	juror
Hill	James	5	1794	29	juror
Hill	James	8	1794	33	juror
Hill	James	2	1795	36	juror

LAST	FIRST	MON	YEAR	PAGE	OTHER
Hill	James	2	1795	41	def
Hill	James	5	1795	43	juror
Hill	James	8	1795	48	juror
Hill	James	8	1795	49	plt
Hill	James	11	1797	94	juror
Hill	James	1	1801	178	def
Hill	John		1792	18	juror
Hill	John		1792	21	def
Hill	John		1792	22	juror
Hill	John	8	1794	33	juror
Hill	John	8	1794	34	juror
Hill	John	8	1794	35	juror
Hill	John	2	1795	38	juror
Hill	John	11	1795	54	juror
Hill	John	5	1796	60	juror
Hill	Joseph	7	1802	206	juror
Hill	Robert	1	1800	159	juror
Hill	Sam	2	1793	110	juror
Hill	Sam	8	1794	33	juror
Hill	Sam	2	1795	37	juror
Hill	Sam	2	1795	42	juror
Hill	Sam	8	1795	48	juror
Hill	Sam	8	1795	48	juror
Hill	Sam Jr.	4	1802	202	juror
Hill	Thomas		1792	2	
Hincle	William		1792	20	bond
Hinny	John	5	1795	44	def
Hixon	Joseph	7	1802	206	plt
Hockdon	Meshack	11	1795	56	juror
Hockdon	Meshack	4	1801	180	plt
Hockton	Mashack	7	1801	187	plt
Hodges	Ambrose	11	1795	52	juror
Hodges	Charles	8	1794	33	plt
Hodges	Charles	8	1794	34	juror
Hodges	Charles	8	1794	35	juror
Hodges	Charles	5	1795	43	plt
Hodges	Charles	8	1795	48	plt
Hodges	Charles	8	1796	63	plt
Hodges	Charles	7	1799	144	plt

JEFFERSON COUNTY TENNESSEE COURT MINUTE BOOKS
INDEX 1783-1816

LAST	FIRST	MON	YEAR	PAGE	OTHER
Hodges	Charles	7	1801	187	def
Hodges	Charles	7	1801	192	def
Hodges	Charles	7	1801	193	def
Hodges	Charles	1	1802	196	def
Hodges	Edmond		1792	12	juror
Hodges	Edmund	2	1797	72	juror
Hodges	Edmund	2	1797	74	juror
Hodges	Edmund	5	1797	82	juror
Hodges	Edmund	8	1797	86	def
Hodges	Edward	7	1800	167	juror
Hodges	James	5	1797	82	juror
Hodges	John		1792	4	
Hodges	John		1792	7	juror
Hodges	John		1792	12	plt
Hodges	John		1792	22	def
Hodges	John	5	1795	44	juror
Hodges	John	8	1795	50	juror
Hodges	John	11	1795	55	juror
Hodges	John	2	1797	72	juror
Hodges	Wm	8	1796	63	juror
Hogan	Raleigh	4	1799	138	juror
Hogan	Raleigh	4	1802	201	juror
Holder	Wm	5	1797	78	def
Homback	James	7	1801	187	juror
Homer	George	1	1800	159	juror
Homer	George	4	1802	204	def
Homer	William	4	1800	164	foreman
Hood	James	8	1797	87	juror
Hooser	Felty	4	1802	202	witness
Hooser	John	11	1797	97	juror
Hopper	Thomas	5	1797	83	victum
Horn	William		1792	8	juror
Horn	William		1792	3	
Horn	William		1792	7	juror
Hornback	John	11	1795	53	juror
Horner	William	5	1794	29	juror
Horner	William	11	1797	98	foreman
Horner	Wm	8	1794	30	juror
Horner	Wm	8	1794	31	juror

JEFFERSON COUNTY TENNESSEE COURT MINUTE BOOKS
INDEX 1783-1816

LAST	FIRST	MON	YEAR	PAGE	OTHER
Horton	Wm	8	1797	90	juror
Hoskins	James	7	1802	206	juror
Hoskins	William	8	1797	88	juror
Hoskins	William	4	1800	164	juror
Hoskins	Wm	8	1795	48	juror
Hoskins	Wm	8	1795	50	juror
Hoskins	Wm	1	1798	109	juror
Hoskins	Wm	1	1798	111	juror
Hoskins	Wm	1	1798	116	juror
Hoskins	Wm	10	1798	130	def
Hoskins	Wm	7	1799	143	plt
Hoskins	Wm	4	1801	180	juror
Hoskins	Wm	1	1802	196	juror
Hoskins	Wm	1	1802	199	juror
House	George	7	1799	141	plt
House	George	7	1801	194	plt
House	George	1	1802	198	plt
House	George [Dec.]	2	1797	74	plt
Housman	Nancy Catrine	4	1799	137	infant victum
Houston	Robert	1	1798	114	plt
Howard	Alexander		1792	19	plt
Howard	John	1	1800	159	juror
Howard	John	7	1801	192	juror
Hudgens	Robert		1792	13	def
Hudgens	Robert	11	1795	52	juror
Huff	Daniel	8	1794	34	juror
Huff	Daniel	8	1794	35	juror
Huff	Sam	11	1795	53	juror
Huff	Sam	11	1795	54	juror
Huges	Abraham		1792	5	juror
Hughes	Aaron	8	1795	49	def
Hughes	Aaron	1	1799	133	plt
Hughes	Abraham		1792	6	juror
Hughes	Abraham		1792	23	juror
Hughes	James		1792	6	juror
Hughes	John	8	1795	50	juror
Hughes	John	8	1795	50	juror
Hughes	Wm		1792	21	juror
Hughes	Wm	5	1794	26	juror

LAST	FIRST	MON	YEAR	PAGE	OTHER
Hume	Jacob		1792	10	juror
Hume	Thomas	1	1798	109	juror
Humes	Thomas	1	1798	110	juror
Humes	Thomas	1	1798	111	juror
Humes	Thomas	1	1798	112	plt
Humpston	Edward	4	1802	201	juror
Hunter	Samuel	11	1797	97	juror
Hurst	John		1792	18	plt
Husk	John		1792	2	
Hutchison	George	5	1797	82	plt
Hynds	George H.	7	1801	187	plt
Hynds	George H.	1	1802	196	plt
Inman	Abednego		1792	10	juror
Inman	Abednego	5	1794	25	juror
Inman	Abednego	5	1794	27	juror
Inman	Abednego	5	1794	27	juror
Inman	Abednego	5	1794	29	juror
Inman	Daniel	8	1794	33	juror
Inman	Daniel	11	1795	53	juror
Inman	Daniel	5	1796	59	juror
Inman	Daniel	8	1796	64	juror
Inman	Daniel	8	1796	64	juror
Inman	David	5	1796	60	def
Inman	George	4	1802	201	def
Inman	Henry	4	1798	120	def
Inman	Henry	7	1798	122	juror
Inman	John	5	1796	60	juror
Inman	John	5	1796	60	def
Inman	John	5	1797	81	def
Inman	John	11	1797	101	juror
Inman	Joseph	4	1798	120	def
Inman	Shadrack		1792	1	
Inman	Shadrack		1792	4	
Inman	Shadrack	5	1794	27	juror
Inman	Shadrack	8	1794	30	juror
Inman	Shadrack	8	1795	50	juror
Inman	Shadrack	5	1796	58	juror
Inman	Shadrick	11	1796	66	juror
Inman	Shadrick	11	1796	69	juror

JEFFERSON COUNTY TENNESSEE COURT MINUTE BOOKS
INDEX 1783-1816

LAST	FIRST	MON	YEAR	PAGE	OTHER
Inman	Shadrick	2	1797	75	plt
Inman	Shadrick	5	1797	78	juror
Inman	Shadrick	8	1797	85	plt
Inman	Shadrick	11	1797	96	juror
Inman	Shadrick	4	1799	135	juror
Inman	Shadrick	1	1801	176	juror
Inman	Shadrick	7	1801	194	def
Inman	Shadrick	1	1802	198	def
Inman	Shandrick	1	1798	106	juror
Inman	William	5	1797	81	def
Inman	Wm	2	1797	70	juror
Inman	Wm	2	1797	71	juror
Inman	Wm	11	1797	97	juror
Inman	Wm	11	1797	99	juror
Inman	Wm	11	1797	100	juror
Inman	Wm	11	1797	101	juror
Inman	Wm	1	1798	107	plt
Inman	Wm	1	1798	115	juror
Inman	Wm	7	1798	123	def
Inman	Wm	7	1799	142	plt
Inman	Wm	7	1799	144	plt
Inman	Wm	1	1801	176	juror
Inskeep	John	7	1799	149	plt
Isham	John	11	1796	68	juror
Ivey	Joel		1792	17	plt
Jack	Sam	2	1793	110	juror
Jack	Sam	8	1795	49	juror
Jack	Sam	8	1795	50	juror
Jack	Sam	8	1795	50	juror
Jack	Sam	11	1795	52	juror
Jack	Sam	5	1796	62	juror
Jack	Sam	8	1796	63	juror
Jack	Sam	11	1796	69	juror
Jack	Sam	8	1797	85	juror
Jack	Sam	4	1798	117	juror
Jack	Sam	7	1798	123	juror
Jack	Samuel		1792	7	juror
Jack	Samuel		1792	14	juror
Jack	Samuel		1792	21	juror

LAST	FIRST	MON	YEAR	PAGE	OTHER
Jack	Samuel		1792	24	juror
Jack	Samuel	7	1798	124	plt
Jackson	Jonah	11	1797	102	def
Jackson	Josiah	7	1799	150	def
Jackson	Samuel	7	1802	206	def
James	Ben	11	1797	99	juror
Jared	William	7	1801	192	juror
Jarnagin	Thomas	2	1797	72	juror
Jarnagin	Thomas	5	1797	78	juror
Jarnagin	Thomas	1	1798	106	juror
Jarnagin	Thomas	1	1798	107	juror
Jarnagin	Thomas	1	1800	159	juror
Jarnagin	Thomas	7	1800	167	juror
Jarrett	Wm	4	1801	180	juror
Jeans	John	5	1795	44	def
Job	Abraham	2	1795	38	juror
Job	Abraham	5	1795	46	juror
Job	Abraham	11	1795	53	plt
Job	Abraham	5	1796	58	def
Job	Abraham	8	1796	63	def
Job	Daniel		1792	9	juror
Job	Sam	2	1795	37	juror
Job	William		1792	20	juror
Job	Wm	2	1795	36	juror
Johns	Ebenezer	10	1798	127	juror
Johnson	Aquilla		1792	12	juror
Johnson	Hugh		1792	11	juror
Johnson	John	8	1794	32	juror
Johnson	John	8	1794	33	juror
Johnson	Michael	2	1793	110	juror
Johnson	Richard	5	1794	27	plt
Johnson	Samuel	4	1802	200	juror
Johnson	William	5	1794	26	juror
Johnson	Wm	5	1794	26	juror
Johnson	Wm	8	1794	32	juror
Johnson	Wm	8	1794	33	juror
Jones	Jesse	4	1799	136	trespass
Jones	Thomas	2	1797	72	juror
Jones	Thomas	11	1797	96	A & B

LAST	FIRST	MON	YEAR	PAGE	OTHER
Jones	Thomas	11	1797	97	victum
Jordan	Mark		1792	7	juror
Jordan	Mark		1792	8	juror
Jordan	Mark		1792	14	juror
Jordan	Mark		1792	15	juror
Kany	Sameul		1792	4	
Kany	Samuel		1792	12	juror
Kany	Thomas		1792	15	plt
Karnes	Adam	8	1797	87	juror
Karnes	Adam	1	1800	160	def
Keen	Jacob		1792	4	
Keene	Jacob	8	1795	50	juror
Keeny	John	5	1795	43	juror
Keeny	Thomas		1792	22	juror
Keith	John	5	1795	46	juror
Kelley	Giles	11	1797	94	juror
Kelley	Giles	1	1798	116	adm-plt
Kelley	Liles	11	1797	93	juror
Kelly	Giles	11	1797	95	juror
Kelly	Giles	7	1798	123	adm-plt
Kelly	Giles	1	1799	132	adm-plt
Kelly	Isaac	5	1797	81	juror
Kelly	Isaac	5	1797	82	juror
Kelly	Isaac	4	1798	117	juror
Kelly	Jacob	4	1799	135	juror
Kelly	Jacob	7	1799	153	juror
Kelly	Sam	7	1799	155	juror
Kelso	Alex		1792	3	
Kelso	Alex		1792	10	juror
Kelso	Alex		1792	21	juror
Kelso	Alex	8	1794	35	juror
Kelso	Alex	2	1795	41	juror
Kelso	Alex	11	1795	53	juror
Kelso	Alex	5	1796	60	juror
Kelso	Alex	2	1797	74	juror
Kelso	Alex	8	1797	89	juror
Kelso	Alex	1	1798	107	juror
Kelso	Alex	7	1798	124	juror
Kelso	Alex	7	1799	157	juror

LAST	FIRST	MON	YEAR	PAGE	OTHER
Kelso	Alexander		1792	1	
Kelso	Alexander	5	1794	26	juror
Kelso	Hugh		1792	21	juror
Kelso	Hugh	5	1794	28	juror
Kelso	Hugh	8	1794	34	juror
Kelso	Hugh	8	1794	35	juror
Kelso	Hugh	5	1795	26	juror
Kelso	Hugh	2	1795	41	juror
Kelso	Hugh	5	1795	43	juror
Kelso	Hugh	11	1795	53	juror
Kelso	Hugh	5	1796	59	juror
Kelso	Hugh	5	1796	60	juror
Kelso	Hugh	5	1796	61	def
Kelso	Hugh	8	1796	64	juror
Kelso	Hugh	8	1797	86	juror
Kelso	Hugh	7	1798	122	juror
Kelson	Ales	4	1801	182	juror
Kelson	Alex		1792	13	juror
Kelson	Alex		1792	24	juror
Kennedy	Daniel	8	1794	34	plt
Kennedy	James		1792	14	plt
Kennedy	Samuel	5	1795	45	plt
Kerr	Andrew	4	1799	139	juror
Kerr	Andrew	4	1800	164	juror
Kerr	Robert		1792	20	juror
Kerry	Thomas		1792	23	juror
Kieth	Thomas	5	1795	44	juror
Kimbro	Jesse	5	1794	27	juror
Kimbro	Jesse	5	1794	27	juror
Kimbro	Jesse	5	1794	29	juror
Kincaid	Thomas	11	1795	54	juror
Kincaid	Thomas	5	1796	60	juror
Kincaid	Thomas	5	1796	62	plt
Kincaid	Thomas	1	1798	106	juror
King	Robert		1792	4	
King	Robert		1792	12	juror
King	Sam	5	1797	79	juror
King	Sam	5	1797	80	juror
King	Sam	11	1797	93	juror

JEFFERSON COUNTY TENNESSEE COURT MINUTE BOOKS
INDEX 1783-1816

LAST	FIRST	MON	YEAR	PAGE	OTHER
King	Sam	11	1797	94	juror
King	Sam	11	1797	95	juror
King	Samuel	5	1797	78	juror
King	Samuel	7	1799	141	def
Kinkaid	Thomas	8	1795	49	juror
Kirkpatric	Hugh		1792	9	juror
Kirkpatrick	James	4	1800	163	juror
Knabb	Jacob	10	1800	173	def
Knabb	Jacob	4	1801	183	def
Knave	Isaac	5	1794	26	juror
Knave	Isaac	2	1795	36	juror
Knave	Isaac	2	1795	38	juror
Knave	John		1792	7	juror
Knave	John		1792	8	juror
Knave	John		1792	9	juror
Knave	John		1792	14	juror
Knave	John		1792	15	juror
Knave	John		1792	15	juror
Knave	John		1792	16	juror
Knave	John		1792	17	juror
Knave	John		1792	18	juror
Knave	John		1792	21	def
Knave	John		1792	22	juror
Knave	John	5	1794	25	juror
Knave	John	5	1794	27	juror
Knave	John	5	1794	29	juror
Knave	John	8	1794	34	juror
Knave	John	8	1794	34	juror
Knave	John	8	1794	35	juror
Knave	John	5	1797	82	juror
Knobb	Jacob	4	1802	200	plt
Krane	John		1792	3	
La Rue	Abraham	7	1801	193	juror
Lackey	James	7	1798	122	plt
Lackey	James W.	5	1795	44	def
Lackey	James W.	11	1795	54	juror
Lake	Joseph	7	1801	190	plt
Lake	Jospeh	4	1801	183	juror
Lambert	Aaron	11	1797	100	juror

LAST	FIRST	MON	YEAR	PAGE	OTHER
Lambert	Aaron	11	1797	101	juror
Lambert	Avery	8	1797	88	larceny
Lambeth	Aaron	11	1797	99	juror
Landsdon	Thomas	2	1795	42	juror
Lane	James	5	1796	60	juror
Lane	Tedana	2	1795	38	juror
Lane	Tidance	8	1794	32	juror
Lane	Tidance	5	1795	43	juror
Lane	Tidence	1	1800	159	juror
Lane	Tidence	7	1800	167	juror
Lane	Tidence	4	1802	204	def
Langdon	Jon Atlas	5	1795	46	juror
Langdon	Jonathan	2	1795	42	plt
Langdon	Jonathan	8	1797	90	A & B
Langdon	Joseph	8	1797	87	victum
Langdon	Joseph	7	1799	145	mismark hogs
Langdon	Joseph	4	1802	201	juror
Larew	Abraham	1	1800	161	juror
Larew	Abraham	4	1800	164	def
Latham	John		1792	19	juror
Layman	David	2	1793	110	juror
Layman	David	2	1795	36	juror
Layman	David	2	1795	38	juror
Layman	David	7	1799	149	juror
Layman	David	4	1800	164	juror
Layman	David	4	1801	182	juror
Layman	David	1	1802	196	juror
Layman	Jacob	2	1795	42	juror
Layman	Jacob	10	1798	129	plt
Laymon	David	5	1795	45	juror
Laymon	Jacob	5	1795	45	juror
Laymon	Jacob	8	1795	48	plt
Laymon	John	8	1795	48	def
Lea	James		1792	18	plt
Lea	James		1792	19	plt
Lea	Major		1792	7	juror
Lea	Major		1792	8	juror
Lea	Major		1792	10	juror
Lea	Major Jr.	4	1802	202	juror

LAST	FIRST	MON	YEAR	PAGE	OTHER
Lea	Peter	8	1795	49	plt
Lea	Peter	11	1797	93	def
Leith	Jonah		1792	23	juror
Leith	Jonah	1	1798	112	juror
Leith	Josiah	7	1799	149	juror
Leith	Josiah	7	1800	172	juror
Leith	Josiah	7	1801	187	juror
Letner	Matthias	10	1800	174	victum
Leuellyn	Richard	11	1797	99	juror
Lewis	Andrew	7	1800	171	def
Lewis	George	1	1800	159	juror
Lewis	James	7	1801	192	plt
Lewis	James	7	1802	206	juror
Ligate	John	5	1795	43	juror
Lillard	James	5	1796	57	juror
Lillard	James	5	1796	58	juror
Lillard	James	8	1797	85	juror
Lillard	James	8	1797	85	juror
Lillard	James	8	1797	89	juror
Lillard	James	11	1797	96	juror
Lillard	William		1792	18	def
Logan	Robert	2	1797	71	plt
Lonacre	Benjamin	4	1802	200	juror
Long	Thomas	5	1795	44	juror
Longacre	Ben	5	1797	77	juror
Longacre	Ben	8	1797	88	juror
Longacre	Ben	1	1798	106	juror
Longacre	Ben	1	1798	107	juror
Longacre	Ben	1	1798	108	juror
Longacre	Ben	1	1798	109	juror
Longacre	Ben	1	1801	176	juror
Longacre	Benjamin	2	1797	72	juror
Love	Wm	1	1800	159	juror
Lowerence	James	4	1802	200	juror
Lowry	Adam	11	1797	94	juror
Lowry	Adam	11	1797	95	juror
Lowry	Robert	5	1797	82	def
Lowry	William		1792	5	def
Lowry	Wm	5	1797	78	exr.-plt

LAST	FIRST	MON	YEAR	PAGE	OTHER
Luellyn	Richard	11	1797	100	juror
Lyle	David		1792	6	juror
Lyle	David		1792	14	juror
Lyle	David		1792	21	juror
Lyle	David	8	1795	50	juror
Lyle	David	5	1796	59	juror
Lyle	David	5	1796	60	juror
Lyle	David	8	1796	64	juror
Lyle	David	8	1796	65	juror
Lyle	David	8	1797	85	juror
Lyle	David	8	1797	89	juror
Lyle	David	1	1798	110	juror
Lyle	David	1	1798	116	juror
Lyle	David	7	1798	122	juror
Lyle	David	4	1802	202	juror
Lyle	Sam	5	1794	26	juror
Lyle	Sam	5	1794	28	juror
Lyle	Sam	8	1794	30	juror
Lyle	Sam	8	1794	31	juror
Lyle	Sam	8	1794	32	juror
Lyle	Sam	8	1794	33	juror
Lyle	Sam	8	1794	34	juror
Lyle	Sam	8	1794	35	juror
Lyle	Sam	2	1795	41	juror
Lyle	Sam	11	1796	68	juror
Lyle	Sam	8	1797	90	juror
Lyle	Sam	1	1798	109	juror
Lyle	Sam	1	1798	112	juror
Lyle	Sam	1	1798	115	juror
Lyle	Sam	4	1798	117	juror
Lyle	Sam	7	1798	124	juror
Lyle	Sam	7	1799	153	juror
Lyle	Sam	1	1802	196	juror
Lyle	Sam	8	2794	34	juror
Lyle	Samuel		1792	12	juror
Lyle	Samuel		1792	21	juror
Lyle	Samuel	5	1794	25	juror
Lyles	Samuel		1792	13	juror
Mabry	Abraham	1	1799	133	def

LAST	FIRST	MON	YEAR	PAGE	OTHER
Mahan	James		1792	13	juror
Mahon	James		1792	9	juror
Mahon	James		1792	14	juror
Mahon	James		1792	15	juror
Majors	Peter	1	1800	159	juror
Majors	Samuel		1792	6	juror
Majors	Samuel		1792	23	juror
Malcom	George	1	1800	159	juror
Malcom	Joseph	1	1799	132	juror
Malcome	George	8	1797	85	juror
Malcome	George	8	1797	87	juror
Maney	Benjamin		1792	12	juror
Maning	Richard	5	1794	29	juror
Maning	Richard	8	1794	30	juror
Maning	Richard	5	1796	57	juror
Maning	Richard	5	1796	58	juror
Mantooth	Thomas	8	1797	87	juror
Manual	Thomas	2	1793	110	juror
Manual	Thomas	2	1795	36	juror
Manual	Thomas	2	1795	38	juror
Manvel	John	8	1797	86	juror
Marshman	Ruth	11	1796	67	w/Hargrove
Martin	John	11	1795	52	def
Massingall	Solomon	5	1795	46	juror
Mathes	Jeremiah	8	1796	63	juror
Mathes	Jeremiah	8	1796	63	juror
Mathes	Jeremiah	5	1797	84	juror
Mathes	Jeremiah	8	1797	85	juror
Mathes	Jeremiah	1	1802	197	foreman
Mathes	Jeremiah	7	1802	208	foreman
Mathes	Obadiah	8	1797	86	juror
Mathes	Sam	8	1797	86	juror
Mathes	Sam	8	1797	89	juror
Mathews	Jeremiah		1792	24	juror
Mathews	Jeremiah	5	1794	27	juror
Mathews	Jeremiah	2	1795	36	juror
Mathews	Jeremiah	1	1801	178	juror
Mathews	Jese		1792	6	juror
Mathews	Mathew		1792	3	

LAST	FIRST	MON	YEAR	PAGE	OTHER
Mathews	Mathew		1792	19	juror
Matthes	Jeremiah	5	1797	77	juror
Matthews	Jeremiah		1792	23	juror
Matthews	Jeremiah		1792	23	def
Matthews	Jeremiah	5	1794	25	juror
Matthews	Jeremiah	11	1795	53	juror
Matthews	Jeremiah	5	1797	78	juror
Matthews	Jeremiah	5	1797	80	juror
Maxwell	John		1792	21	juror
Maxwell	John	7	1799	154	plt
Maxwell	John	7	1800	167	juror
Maxwell	John	1	1801	176	juror
May	Samuel	5	1797	79	plt
Mayberry	Frederick		1792	9	juror
Mayberry	Frederick		1792	11	juror
Mayberry	Frederick		1792	16	plt
Mayberry	George	8	1797	93	def
Mayberry	John		1792	7	juror
Mayberry	John		1792	9	larceny
Mayberry	John		1792	11	affray
Mc Peters	David		1792	5	juror
Mc Affey	Terence	1	1801	178	plt
Mc Alister	Wm	7	1799	157	juror
Mc Cag	Wm	11	1797	100	juror
Mc Cagg	William	5	1794	26	plt
Mc Cagg	William	1	1798	116	plt
Mc Cagg	William	7	1798	121	plt
Mc Cagg	Wm	5	1797	78	juror
Mc Cagg	Wm	11	1797	101	juror
Mc Cagg	Wm	1	1798	116	plt
Mc Cally	John	1	1799	132	juror
Mc Cammon	Robert	8	1796	64	plt
Mc Clanaha	John		1792	12	juror
Mc Clanahan	David	8	1797	88	juror
Mc Clanahan	James	7	1798	124	def
Mc Clanahan	John	8	1797	92	def
Mc Clure	Robert	4	1801	183	plt
Mc Connell	Joseph	5	1797	80	plt
Mc Connell	Joseph	11	1797	99	plt

LAST	FIRST	MON	YEAR	PAGE	OTHER
Mc Corry	Crozier	1	1802	196	plt
Mc Cown	George		1792	10	juror
Mc Cown	George		1792	12	juror
Mc Cown	George		1792	13	juror
Mc Cown	George		1792	14	juror
Mc Cown	George		1792	17	juror
Mc Cown	George		1792	18	juror
Mc Cown	George		1792	20	juror
Mc Cown	George		1792	20	juror
Mc Cown	James		1792	14	plt
Mc Cuistion	Andrew	2	1797	74	juror
Mc Cuistion	James	4	1802	201	juror
Mc Cullah	Joseph	4	1801	180	juror
Mc Donald	Alex		1792	19	juror
Mc Donald	Alexander		1792	15	juror
Mc Donald	Alexander		1792	16	juror
Mc Donald	Alexander		1792	17	juror
Mc Donald	Alexander		1792	18	juror
Mc Donald	James	11	1795	52	juror
Mc Donald	James	4	1802	202	juror
Mc Donald	John	4	1799	135	juror
Mc Donald	John	1	1801	176	juror
Mc Donald	Randolph		1792	9	juror
Mc Donald	Randolph		1792	14	juror
Mc Donald	Randolph		1792	15	juror
Mc Donald	Randolph		1792	16	juror
Mc Donald	Randolph		1792	17	juror
Mc Donald	Randolph		1792	18	juror
Mc Donald	Randolph		1792	19	juror
Mc Donald	Randolph	5	1794	27	juror
Mc Donald	Randolph	5	1794	29	juror
Mc Donald	Randolph	8	1797	90	A & B
Mc Donald	Walter	2	1797	75	juror
Mc Donals	Randolph		1792	12	juror
Mc Dowell	James		1792	13	larceny
Mc Dowell	James		1792	21	juror
Mc Dowell	James		1792	22	juror
Mc Dowell	James		1792	23	def
Mc Dowell	James	8	1794	33	juror

LAST	FIRST	MON	YEAR	PAGE	OTHER
Mc Dowell	James	8	1794	35	plt
Mc Dowell	James	8	1794	35	juror
Mc Dowell	John		1792	12	juror
Mc Elheny	Moses	11	1795	53	def
Mc Farland	Daniel	8	1796	63	juror
Mc Farland	Edward	8	1794	32	robery
Mc Farland	Edward	5	1797	77	def
Mc Farland	Edward	5	1797	77	plt
Mc Farland	George	11	1796	69	juror
Mc Farland	George	2	1797	72	juror
Mc Farland	Jacob	8	1794	33	juror
Mc Farland	John		1792	3	
Mc Farland	John		1792	23	juror
Mc Farland	John	8	1794	33	juror
Mc Farland	John	8	1794	34	juror
Mc Farland	John	8	1794	35	juror
Mc Farland	John	2	1795	36	juror
Mc Farland	John	2	1795	41	plt
Mc Farland	John	2	1795	42	juror
Mc Farland	John	5	1795	43	juror
Mc Farland	John	2	1797	70	juror
Mc Farland	John	2	1797	71	juror
Mc Farland	John	2	1797	75	juror
Mc Farland	John	5	1797	81	juror
Mc Farland	John	4	1800	163	juror
Mc Farland	Robert		1792	13	plt
Mc Gairy	Samuel		1792	18	juror
Mc Gee	Barclay	8	1795	51	plt
Mc Gee	Barkley	7	1799	153	plt
Mc Gee	John	7	1800	172	juror
Mc Ghee	James	5	1795	43	juror
Mc Girt	John		1792	4	
Mc Girt	John	5	1794	25	juror
Mc Girt	John	2	1795	38	juror
Mc Girt	John	11	1795	53	juror
Mc Girt	John	5	1796	60	juror
Mc Girt	John	7	1798	121	juror
Mc Girt	John	1	1800	159	juror
Mc Girt	John	7	1800	166	juror

LAST	FIRST	MON	YEAR	PAGE	OTHER
Mc Gist	John		1792	7	juror
Mc Gist	John		1792	8	juror
Mc Gown	Andrew		1792	12	juror
Mc Gown	Andrew		1792	23	juror
Mc Gown	Andrew	8	1795	50	juror
Mc Gown	Andrew	2	1797	74	juror
Mc Gown	Andrew	4	1799	139	juror
Mc Gown	Andrew	7	1799	141	juror
Mc Gown	Andrew	7	1799	142	juror
Mc Guire	Cornelius	8	1797	85	juror
Mc Guire	Cornelius	7	1798	123	juror
Mc Guire	Cornelius	7	1798	124	juror
Mc Guire	Cornelius	7	1799	155	juror
Mc Guire	Cornelius	4	1801	180	juror
Mc Guire	George	11	1795	52	juror
Mc Guire	Neeley		1792	3	
Mc Guire	Neely	2	1795	36	juror
Mc Guire	Neely	2	1795	37	juror
Mc Guire	Neely	11	1795	56	juror
Mc Guire	Patrick	1	1802	196	juror
Mc Guirt	John	5	1797	77	juror
Mc Guirt	John	4	1799	139	juror
Mc Holm	Wm	4	1799	135	juror
Mc Kay	Andrew	4	1799	135	plt
Mc Kinney	Rollin		1792	21	juror
Mc Kinny	Augustus	8	1797	86	A & B
Mc Kinny	Rolin	11	1797	99	juror
Mc Kinny	Rollin	11	1795	55	juror
Mc Kinny	Rollin	5	1797	81	juror
Mc Kinny	Rollin	1	1798	108	plt
Mc Kinny	Rowlin	8	1797	86	A & B
Mc Lister	James	4	1802	201	juror
Mc Long	John	1	1799	133	def
Mc Mahan	Wm	11	1795	55	juror
Mc Mean	Isaac	7	1799	153	juror
Mc Mean	Isaac	7	1799	155	juror
Mc Mean	Isaac	7	1801	193	juror
Mc Mean	John	7	1799	155	juror
Mc Means	Isaac	7	1798	121	juror

JEFFERSON COUNTY TENNESSEE COURT MINUTE BOOKS
INDEX 1783-1816

LAST	FIRST	MON	YEAR	PAGE	OTHER
Mc Means	Isaac	1	1802	196	juror
Mc Means	John	7	1802	206	juror
Mc Means	Nathan	8	1797	89	juror
Mc Neely	Robert		1792	9	juror
Mc Neely	Robert		1792	11	juror
Mc Neely	Robert		1792	14	juror
Mc Neely	Robert		1792	22	juror
Mc Neely	Robert	5	1794	27	juror
Mc Neely	Robert	5	1794	28	plt
Mc Neely	Robert	5	1796	62	juror
Mc Neely	Robert	8	1796	63	juror
Mc Neely	Robert	11	1796	69	juror
Mc Niel	John		1792	17	juror
Mc Peters	David		1792	3	
Mc Peters	David		1792	4	
Mc Peters	David		1792	6	juror
Mc Peters	David		1792	8	def
Mc Peters	J.	8	1797	85	def
Mc Puton	David		1792	2	
Mc Roberts	Samuel	1	1799	132	juror
Mc Spadden	Archi	7	1799	157	juror
Mc Spadden	Archibald	8	1797	85	juror
Mc Spadden	Archibald	1	1798	116	juror
Mc Spadden	Archibald	1	1799	134	def
Mc Spadden	John		1792	3	
Mc Spadden	John		1792	6	juror
Mc Spadden	John	5	1797	84	juror
Mc Spadden	Moses	1	1798	109	juror
Mc Spadden	Sam		1792	5	juror
Mc Spadden	Sam	5	1797	81	juror
Mc Spadden	Samuel		1792	6	juror
Mc Wallace	Ben		1792	18	juror
Medingall	Martin	7	1800	167	juror
Meed	Adam	5	1794	26	exr-def
Meek	A. [Deceased	11	1795	54	plt
Meek	Adam		1792	9	def
Meek	Adam		1792	17	def
Meek	Adam		1792	18	def
Meek	Adam		1792	19	def

JEFFERSON COUNTY TENNESSEE COURT MINUTE BOOKS
INDEX 1783-1816

LAST	FIRST	MON	YEAR	PAGE	OTHER
Meek	Adam		1792	20	plt
Meek	Adam	2	1797	70	plt
Menarco	James	8	1794	33	def
Menasco	James		1792	16	juror
Menasco	James		1792	17	juror
Mendenall	Martin	1	1798	110	juror
Mendinall	Martin	1	1798	111	juror
Mendingall	Joseph	1	1801	177	juror
Mendingall	Martin	1	1798	110	juror
Mendingall	Martin	1	1798	112	juror
Mendingall	Martin	7	1799	151	juror
Mendingall	Martin	7	1799	156	juror
Mendingall	Martin	1	1800	161	juror
Mendingall	Mordecai	5	1797	80	juror
Michaels	Barney	10	1798	126	juror
Millard	John		1792	4	
Millen	John	7	1801	192	juror
Miller	Robert	11	1795	55	plt
Miller	Wm	7	1801	193	def
Miller	Wm	1	1802	199	def
Millican	James		1792	14	juror
Milliken	James		1792	15	plt
Milller	Robert	1	1802	199	juror
Mills	John	7	1799	156	juror
Minarco	James		1792	22	juror
Minasco	James		1792	24	juror
Mitchell	James		1792	8	juror
Mitchell	James		1792	14	juror
Mitchell	James		1792	15	def
Mitchell	James		1792	21	plt
Mitchell	Mark		1792	21	plt
Moderal	George	5	1795	45	def
Moderal	George	1	1798	109	juror
Moderal	George	7	1799	150	def
Moffett	William		1792	23	juror
Moffett	William	1	1798	111	plt
Moffett	Wm	7	1800	166	plt
Moffett	Wm	4	1801	182	plt
Monroe	James		1792	23	juror

LAST	FIRST	MON	YEAR	PAGE	OTHER
Monroe	William		1792	14	juror
Montgomery	Alex		1792	3	
Montgomery	Alex		1792	4	
Montgomery	Alex		1792	5	juror
Montgomery	Alex		1792	6	juror
Montgomery	Alex		1792	15	juror
Montgomery	Alex		1792	16	juror
Montgomery	Alex		1792	18	juror
Montgomery	Alex		1792	18	juror
Montgomery	Alex	5	1794	27	juror
Montgomery	Alex	5	1794	27	juror
Montgomery	Alex	5	1795	44	juror
Montgomery	Alex	5	1795	46	juror
Montgomery	Alex	8	1795	49	juror
Montgomery	Alexander		1792	3	
Montgomery	Alexander		1792	10	juror
Montgomery	Alexander		1792	17	juror
Montgomery	James	1	1801	178	juror
Montgomery	John		1792	3	
Montgomery	John		1792	3	
Montgomery	Joseph	2	1795	38	juror
Montgomery	Michael		1792	5	juror
Montgomery	Michael		1792	6	juror
Montgomery	Michael	2	1795	37	juror
Montgomery	Michael	2	1795	38	juror
Montgomery	Michael	5	1795	47	plt
Montgomery	Michael	8	1795	48	juror
Montgomery	Michael	8	1795	49	juror
Montgomery	Michael	8	1795	51	juror
Montgomery	Michael	11	1795	55	juror
Montgomery	Michael	5	1797	84	juror
Montgomery	Michael	7	1798	121	juror
Montgomery	Michael	1	1800	159	juror
Montgomery	Michael	4	1801	183	juror
Montgomery	William		1792	6	juror
Montgomery	William	4	1800	163	overseer
Montgomery	Wm	2	1795	42	juror
Montgomery	Wm	7	1801	192	juror
Moon	James		1792	2	plt

LAST	FIRST	MON	YEAR	PAGE	OTHER
Moore	Anthony	7	1799	153	juror
Moore	Ben	11	1795	52	juror
Moore	Robert	7	1798	123	juror
Moore	Sam	2	1795	37	juror
Moore	Samuel	11	1795	53	plt
Mopper ?	Thomas	10	1798	126	juror
Morgan	Richard	1	1798	111	juror
Morgan	Silas	7	1799	142	juror
Morgan	Silas	7	1799	149	juror
Morris	Gid	8	1795	48	juror
Morris	Gideon		1792	7	juror
Morris	Gideon		1792	7	juror
Morris	Gideon		1792	8	juror
Morris	Gideon		1792	10	juror
Morris	Gideon		1792	21	juror
Morris	Gideon	5	1794	25	def
Morris	Gideon	5	1795	44	juror
Morris	Gideon	11	1796	69	juror
Morris	Gideon	2	1797	71	juror
Morris	Gideon	2	1797	74	def
Morris	John	8	1796	63	juror
Morris	John	11	1797	97	juror
Morris	John	4	1799	138	juror
Morris	Junot	7	1801	193	adm-plt
Morris	Robert	7	1799	149	def
Morriss	Gideon		1792	16	def
Morrow	David	4	1802	201	juror
Morrow	John		1792	12	juror
Morrow	John	2	1795	37	juror
Morrow	John	5	1796	59	juror
Morrow	John	8	1797	90	juror
Morrow	John	1	1798	109	juror
Morrow	John	1	1798	116	juror
Morrow	John	10	1798	127	juror
Morrow	William		1792	13	juror
Morrow	William		1792	20	juror
Morrow	William		1792	20	juror
Morrow	William		1792	22	juror
Morrow	Wm	5	1795	43	juror

LAST	FIRST	MON	YEAR	PAGE	OTHER
Morrow	Wm	11	1795	54	juror
Morrow	Wm	11	1795	54	juror
Morrow	Wm	5	1796	57	juror
Morrow	Wm	2	1797	74	juror
Morrow	Wm	5	1797	77	juror
Morrow	Wm	5	1797	84	juror
Morrow	Wm	7	1798	121	juror
Morrow	Wm	7	1800	171	def
Moulder	Henry	10	1798	126	juror
Moulder	Henry	7	1800	167	juror
Moulder	John	7	1798	121	juror
Moulder	John	10	1798	126	juror
Moulder	Valentine	10	1798	126	juror
Moyers	Adam	1	1801	178	juror
Moyers	David	7	1798	122	juror
Moyers	David	7	1801	192	juror
Moyers	James	8	1797	85	juror
Moyers	James	11	1797	96	juror
Moyers	Joshua	7	1798	122	juror
Murphy	John	4	1799	136	juror
Murphy	John	4	1799	140	def
Murrell	Ben	5	1795	44	juror
Murrell	Ben	1	1799	132	juror
Nancy	Robert W.		1792	8	plt
Nave	John	8	1797	93	def
Nave	John	11	1797	93	juror
Neely	Andrew	2	1795	41	juror
Neely	Andrew	5	1795	43	plt
Neely	Andrew	5	1796	57	juror
Neely	Andrew	5	1796	58	juror
Neely	Andrew	5	1796	60	juror
Neely	Andrew	7	1802	206	juror
Neely	James		1792	16	juror
Neely	James	8	1797	90	juror
Neely	James	11	1797	96	juror
Neely	James	1	1798	114	def
Neely	John	5	1794	29	juror
Neely	John	8	1794	30	juror
Neely	John	8	1794	34	juror

JEFFERSON COUNTY TENNESSEE COURT MINUTE BOOKS
INDEX 1783-1816

LAST	FIRST	MON	YEAR	PAGE	OTHER
Neely	John	5	1795	43	juror
Neely	John	5	1795	45	juror
Neely	John	5	1795	45	def
Neely	John	5	1796	60	juror
Neely	John	7	1800	171	plt
Neely	Robert	5	1794	29	juror
Neely	Robert W.	5	1794	26	juror
Neely	Sam	1	1800	159	juror
Nelson	William		1792	12	juror
Nelson	Wm	11	1795	53	juror
Nelson	Wm	2	1797	71	juror
Nelson	Wm	5	1797	81	plt
Nelson	Wm	1	1800	161	juror
Netherton	John	5	1796	60	def
Netherton	John	1	1798	115	def
Newman	Isaac	5	1797	77	juror
Newman	Isaac	8	1797	87	juror
Newman	Isaac	8	1797	89	juror
Newman	Isaac	11	1797	95	juror
Newman	Isaac	11	1797	98	assault
Newman	Isaac	11	1797	99	juror
Newman	Isaac	1	1798	106	juror
Newman	Isaac	1	1798	107	juror
Newman	Isaac	1	1798	108	juror
Newman	Isaac	1	1798	109	A & B
Newman	Isaac	1	1798	110	juror
Newman	Isaac	1	1798	111	juror
Newman	Isaac	1	1798	112	juror
Newman	Isaac	7	1799	157	juror
Newman	Isaac	4	1802	200	juror
Newman	Isaac	4	1802	201	trespass
Newman	Isaac	4	1802	202	juror
Newman	Joseph	1	1802	199	juror
Nicholson	Jeremiah	11	1797	94	juror
Nicholson	Jeremiah	11	1797	95	juror
Nicholson	John	7	1799	149	def
Nicholson	Joseph	1	1798	107	juror
Nicholson	Joseph	1	1798	107	juror
Nicholson	Joseph	1	1798	108	juror

LAST	FIRST	MON	YEAR	PAGE	OTHER
Nicholson	Joseph	1	1802	199	juror
Nickers	James	8	1794	31	juror
Oats	Roger		1792	11	juror
Odle	Jonathan	1	1801	178	juror
Osten	Archibald	1	1798	106	juror
Ostin	Archi	11	1797	93	juror
Ostin	Archi	11	1797	94	juror
Ostin	Archi	11	1797	96	juror
Ostin	Archi	1	1798	107	juror
Ostin	Archi	1	1798	108	juror
Ostin	Archibald	11	1797	95	juror
Ostin	Archibald	1	1798	109	juror
Outlaw	Alexander	2	1793	110	plt
Outlaw	Alexander	2	1795	42	plt
Outlaw	Alexander	11	1797	105	def
Paggett	John		1792	18	juror
Parker	Abraham	10	1798	131	def
Parker	Abraham	1	1801	177	def
Parker	Philip	5	1796	60	juror
Parks	William		1792	2	
Parks	William		1792	11	victum
Parks	Wm	2	1795	41	plt
Parks	Wm	8	1796	63	juror
Patton	Robert		1792	7	juror
Patton	Robert		1792	12	juror
Patton	Robert		1792	14	juror
Patton	Robert	11	1796	68	juror
Patton	Robert	2	1797	71	juror
Patton	Robert	2	1797	72	juror
Patton	Robert	5	1797	78	juror
Patton	Robert	5	1797	79	juror
Patton	Robert	5	1797	80	juror
Patton	Robert	7	1799	154	def
Patton	Sam		1792	3	
Payne	Enoch	7	1799	155	def
Payne	Samuel		1792	7	plt
Peery	John	2	1797	74	juror
Pepper	John		1792	11	juror
Pepper	John		1792	12	juror

LAST	FIRST	MON	YEAR	PAGE	OTHER
Pepper	John		1792	14	juror
Pepper	John		1792	15	juror
Pepper	John		1792	21	juror
Pepper	John	8	1794	35	juror
Pepper	John	8	1795	50	juror
Pepper	John	8	1795	50	juror
Pepper	John	11	1795	52	juror
Pepper	John	11	1795	56	juror
Pepper	John	5	1796	57	juror
Perry	George	5	1794	29	plt
Perry	Wm	8	1796	63	juror
Perryman	Benoni	5	1796	59	juror
Perryman	Benoni	2	1797	70	juror
Perryman	Benoni	2	1797	71	juror
Perryman	Benoni	5	1797	78	juror
Perryman	Benoni	5	1797	81	juror
Perryman	Benoni	8	1797	85	juror
Perryman	Benoni	8	1797	87	juror
Perryman	Benoni	11	1797	103	def
Perryman	Benoni	7	1800	166	def
Perryman	Benoni	4	1802	200	def
Petty	John	1	1799	133	plt
Phares	Samuel	1	1798	116	def
Pharice	Samuel	7	1798	123	def
Pharice	Samuel	1	1799	132	def
Pharice	Samuel	4	1799	135	def
Pharis	John	8	1797	90	juror
Pharis	Sam	11	1797	99	juror
Pharis	Samuel	8	1797	87	juror
Phenix	Mathew	7	1798	121	def
Philips	Edward	4	1799	136	juror
Pickens	James	5	1797	80	plt
Pohon	Wm	1	1798	107	juror
Porter	Charles	8	194	32	juror
Porter	Charles	8	1794	33	juror
Porter	Charles	7	1799	149	plt
Preston	Francis	1	1800	161	plt
Price	Ralph	7	1800	172	juror
Priddy	Richard	5	1795	43	def

LAST	FIRST	MON	YEAR	PAGE	OTHER
Priddy	Richard	11	1795	55	juror
Priddy	Richard	5	1796	60	juror
Priddy	Richard	4	1799	138	juror
Priddy	Richard	4	1799	140	plt
Priddy	Richard	7	1799	149	juror
Prigmore	John	4	1801	181	witness
Prigmore	Joseph	4	1801	181	victum
Ramsey	Francis A.		1792	8	plt
Rankin	Richard	8	1794	30	juror
Rankin	Richard	4	1802	200	juror
Rankin	Sam	7	1799	155	juror
Rankin	Sam	1	1802	196	juror
Rankin	Samuel	1	1799	132	juror
Rankin	Thomas	1	1798	110	juror
Rankin	Thomas	4	1802	200	juror
Raulston	Moses		1792	18	juror
Raulstone	Sam	7	1801	192	juror
Rector	Uriah	5	1797	80	def
Reddick	William	4	1799	136	plt
Reese	Thomas	7	1801	193	juror
Regan	Henry	2	1797	70	juror
Reneau	Thomas	4	1802	202	juror
Renfrow	Isaac		1792	20	plt
Renfrow	John		1792	16	juror
Renfrow	John	8	1794	33	juror
Renfrow	John	8	1794	34	juror
Renfrow	John	8	1794	35	def
Renfrow	John	11	1795	55	def
Renno	George	11	1797	101	juror
Renno	John	5	1795	47	def
Renno	John	4	1799	138	juror
Renno	John	1	1800	159	juror
Renno	Thomas		1792	17	def
Renno	Thomas		1792	21	juror
Renno	Thomas	2	1795	41	juror
Renno	Thomas	5	1795	44	juror
Renno	Thomas	8	1795	51	juror
Renno	Thomas	7	1798	124	juror
Renno	Thomas	1	1799	132	juror

LAST	FIRST	MON	YEAR	PAGE	OTHER
Renno	Thomas	7	1799	143	def
Renno	Thomas	7	1800	172	juror
Renno	Thomas	10	1800	173	plt
Reyburn	John	5	1794	28	plt
Rhea	George	7	1799	151	juror
Rhea	George	7	1800	172	juror
Rhea	George	4	1801	183	juror
Rhea	George	1	1802	199	juror
Rhea	John		1792	1	
Rhea	John	7	1800	172	plt
Rice	Daniel		1792	2	
Richardson	James	8	1795	51	juror
Riddle	John	8	1794	30	juror
Rider	Reuben	11	1795	53	def
Riggs	Clisby		1792	21	plt
Riggs	Clisby	2	1793	110	plt
Riggs	Clisby	5	1796	57	juror
Riggs	Clisby	5	1796	58	juror
Riggs	Edward	5	1795	43	juror
Riggs	Edward	5	1796	57	juror
Riggs	Edward	5	1796	58	juror
Riggs	Edward	5	1797	78	juror
Riggs	Edward	5	1797	81	juror
Riggs	Jesse	8	1795	52	
Riggs	Jesse	5	1797	82	juror
Riggs	Jesse	11	1797	97	juror
Riggs	Jesse	1	1798	110	juror
Riggs	Jesse	4	1798	119	plt
Rite	John	1	1798	109	juror
Roach	Jordan	7	1800	167	def
Roach	Reuben		1792	1	burglary
Roane	Henry		1792	21	juror
Roane	Henry	2	1795	36	victum
Roane ?	John	4	1799	135	juror
Roberts	James	2	1797	75	affray
Roberts	John		1792	8	juror
Roberts	John M.		1792	7	juror
Roberts	Phillip	2	1795	41	juror
Robinson	Joseph		1792	3	

LAST	FIRST	MON	YEAR	PAGE	OTHER
Robinson	Joseph		1792	4	
Robinson	Joseph		1792	17	juror
Robinson	Joseph	11	1795	54	juror
Robinson	Joseph	5	1796	57	juror
Robinson	Joseph	5	1796	57	def
Robinson	Joseph	5	1796	58	juror
Robinson	Joseph	5	1796	60	def
Robinson	Joseph	5	1797	80	def
Robinson	Wm	11	1795	52	juror
Roddy	James	7	1799	156	plt
Roddye	James	4	1800	163	plt
Roddye	James	4	1801	186	plt
Rodgers	Ben	8	1794	32	juror
Rodgers	Bery		1792	6	juror
Rodgers	George	2	1795	38	juror
Rodgers	George	2	1795	42	juror
Rodgers	George	5	1795	43	juror
Rodgers	Hugh		1792	23	juror
Rodgers	Isaac	5	1795	43	juror
Rodgers	Isaac	11	1795	55	juror
Rodgers	Isaac W.	7	1800	167	plt
Rodgers	Jonah	5	1794	28	juror
Rodgers	Josiah	5	1794	28	plt
Rodgers	Larkin		1792	23	plt
Rodgers	Robert		1792	21	juror
Rodgers	Robert		1792	23	juror
Rodgers	Thomas	5	1795	43	juror
Rogers	Ben	5	1794	26	juror
Rogers	Elijah		1792	22	juror
Rogers	Isaac		1792	12	juror
Rogers	Isaac		1792	14	juror
Rogers	Isaac		1792	15	juror
Rogers	Isaac	8	1797	85	juror
Rogers	Isaac	8	1797	88	juror
Rogers	Isaac W.	1	1800	160	plt
Rogers	Robert		1792	22	juror
Rogers	Stephen	7	1799	146	riot
Romine	Sam	1	1800	161	juror
Rorax	Wm	7	1799	144	def

LAST	FIRST	MON	YEAR	PAGE	OTHER
Rose	Benjamin	11	1797	105	def
Rose	Benjamin	1	1798	116	juror
Rosey	Samuel		1792	22	juror
Ross	James	8	1794	30	juror
Roulston	Wm	1	1800	161	juror
Roulstone	James	4	1802	201	juror
Roulstone	Moses	1	1802	196	def
Roulstone	Wm	4	1802	201	juror
Routstone	Moses	4	1802	200	plt
Rowan	Henry		1792	19	juror
Rush	Jeremiah	11	1797	96	juror
Russell	Andrew		1792	15	juror
Russell	Andrew		1792	16	juror
Russell	Andrew		1792	20	juror
Russell	Andrew	2	1797	74	juror
Russell	Andrew	11	1797	96	juror
Russell	Andrew	7	1800	169	def
Russell	Andrew	4	1801	180	def
Russell	Andrew	4	1801	183	juror
Russell	Andrew	7	1801	187	def
Russell	Daniel	2	1795	36	juror
Russell	Daniel	2	1795	37	juror
Russell	David	1	1802	196	juror
Russell	Gilbert	1	1802	199	juror
Russell	James	4	1799	135	juror
Rynehart	Michael	4	1801	183	juror
Salvage	Patrick	2	1793	110	juror
Salvage	Patrick	5	1794	28	juror
Salvage	Patrick	5	1796	60	juror
Salvage	Patrick	7	1799	156	juror
Samples	Mathew	7	1802	206	juror
Samples	Moses		1792	15	juror
Samples	Moses		1792	16	juror
Samples	Moses		1792	17	juror
Samples	William	1	1800	161	juror
Sandusky	Jacob	5	1794	26	juror
Sandusky	Jacob	8	1794	35	juror
Sandusky	Jacob	5	1797	81	juror
Schornand	John	8	1796	65	juror

LAST	FIRST	MON	YEAR	PAGE	OTHER
Scott	Edward	8	1797	92	plt
Scott	James	5	1795	43	juror
Scott	James	5	1796	58	juror
Scott	James	8	1797	89	juror
Scott	James	1	1800	159	juror
Scott	James	7	1800	171	def
Scott	James	1	1801	178	juror
Scott	James	4	1802	201	juror
Scott	Joseph	11	1796	69	juror
Seaborn	Edward	5	1797	81	juror
Seaborn	Edward	7	1800	167	juror
Seaborne	Edward	8	1795	50	juror
Seaborne	Edward	5	1797	78	juror
Seebourn	Edward	5	1795	43	juror
Seehorn	John		1792	10	juror
Seehorn	John		1792	15	juror
Seehorn	John		1792	16	juror
Seehorn	John	5	1794	27	juror
Seehorn	John	5	1794	29	juror
Seehorn	John	11	1795	53	juror
Seehorn	John	8	1796	64	juror
Seehorn	John	8	1797	85	juror
Sellers	John	4	1800	164	juror
Sellers	Sam	7	1801	192	juror
Sellers	Thomas		1792	22	juror
Selvey	Jacob	1	1798	110	juror
Selvey	Jacob	1	1798	111	juror
Selvey	Jacob	1	1798	112	juror
Selvy	Wm	11	1797	96	juror
Sephenson	Edward	2	1795	42	juror
Sevier	John		1792	3	def
Sevier	John		1792	9	def
Sevier	John		1792	17	def
Sevier	John		1792	18	def
Sevier	John		1792	19	def
Sevier	John	5	1794	26	exr-def
Sevier	John	5	1796	58	plt
Sevier	John	2	1797	70	plt
Shadden	Alex	2	1797	74	juror

LAST	FIRST	MON	YEAR	PAGE	OTHER
Shadden	Alex	2	1797	75	juror
Shadden	Alex	5	1797	84	juror
Shadden	James		1792	23	juror
Shadden	James		1792	24	juror
Shadden	James	5	1794	27	juror
Shadden	James	8	1794	32	juror
Shadden	James	2	1795	38	juror
Shadden	James	5	1795	45	juror
Shadden	James	8	1795	51	juror
Shadden	James	11	1795	56	juror
Shadden	James	2	1797	74	juror
Shadden	James	5	1797	84	juror
Shadden	James	1	1800	161	juror
Shadden	John		1792	3	
Shadden	John		1792	16	juror
Shadden	John		1792	17	juror
Shadden	John		1792	20	juror
Shadden	John	5	1794	28	juror
Shadden	John	8	1794	31	juror
Shadden	John	2	1795	38	juror
Shadden	John	11	1795	56	juror
Shadden	Thomas		1792	3	
Shadden	Thomas		1792	6	juror
Shadden	Thomas	11	1796	68	juror
Shane	John	2	1797	75	juror
Shanks	Holden	7	1799	152	plt
Shanks	Nicholas	7	1801	190	def
Shelly	Jeremiah	1	1799	132	juror
Shelly	Jeremiah	7	1800	166	juror
Shelly	Wm	7	1798	124	def
Shelton	James	2	1797	74	juror
Shelton	James	4	1799	135	juror
Shelton	Thomas	5	1795	43	juror
Shelton	Thomas	5	1796	58	juror
Shelton	Thomas	2	1797	74	juror
Shelton	Thomas	7	1798	121	juror
Shelton	Thomas	7	1798	122	juror
Shelton	Thomas	7	1801	194	def
Shelton	Thomas	1	1802	198	def

JEFFERSON COUNTY TENNESSEE COURT MINUTE BOOKS
INDEX 1783-1816

LAST	FIRST	MON	YEAR	PAGE	OTHER
Shetley	Wm	11	1797	94	def
Shield	John	8	1795	51	juror
Shields	David	8	1794	34	juror
Shields	David	8	1794	34	def
Shields	David	10	1800	173	def
Shields	Ebenezer	7	1802	206	juror
Shields	John	5	1796	57	adm.-def
Shields	John	2	1797	76	
Shields	John	5	1797	79	adm-def
Shields	John	7	1798	122	def
Shields	John [Dec.]	11	1796	69	plt
Shields	John [Deceased]	7	1799	154	plt
Shinall	Isaac	8	1794	30	juror
Shinall	Isaac	8	1794	33	juror
Shinall	Isaac	2	1797	74	juror
Shinall	Isaac	2	1797	75	juror
Shinall	Isaac	5	1797	77	juror
Shinall	Isaac	1	1798	109	juror
Shinall	Isaac	1	1798	115	juror
Silvey	Wm	11	1797	99	juror
Simmons	Reuben	5	1797	79	juror
Simmons	Reuben	5	1797	84	victum
Simmons	Robert	5	1797	79	juror
Sims	Job	11	1796	68	juror
Sims	Job	11	1797	99	juror
Sively	Jacob	2	1795	42	juror
Skeen	John	5	1796	59	juror
Skeen	John	2	1797	74	juror
Skeen	John	10	1798	127	juror
Skeen	John & Fen	11	1796	69	def
Skeene	Jacob	5	1794	26	juror
Skeene	John	5	1797	83	juror
Skeene	John	1	1798	107	juror
Skeene	John	1	1798	108	juror
Skeene	John	1	1798	110	juror
Skeene	John	7	1799	154	def
Skeene	John	7	1800	166	juror
Slover	Abraham	2	1795	38	juror
Slover	Abraham	8	1796	63	juror

LAST	FIRST	MON	YEAR	PAGE	OTHER
Slover	Abraham	8	1796	63	juror
Small	Willaim		1792	14	juror
Small	William		1792	23	def
Small	William	11	1797	105	def
Small	Wm		1792	23	juror
Small	Wm	8	1794	30	def
Small	Wm	5	1795	45	juror
Small	Wm	8	1795	49	juror
Small	Wm	8	1796	64	def
Small	Wm	2	1797	72	juror
Small	Wm	2	1797	74	juror
Small	Wm	2	1797	75	juror
Small	Wm	8	1797	91	def
Small	Wm	11	1797	99	def
Small	Wm	11	1797	100	def
Small	Wm	11	1797	104	def
Small	Wm	1	1798	106	def
Small	Wm	10	1798	129	def
Small	Wm	4	1800	163	def
Smith	Gideon		1792	8	juror
Smith	Margaret	7	1799	151	plt
Smith	Margaret	1	1800	159	plt
Smith	Samuel		1792	24	adm.-def
Smith	Samuel	11	1796	65	dec
Smith	Thomas	7	1801	193	juror
Smith	Thomas	4	1802	201	trespass
Smith	Willaim		1792	24	adm.-plt
Smith	William		1792	4	burglary
Smith	Wm	11	1797	95	def
Smith	Wm	1	1798	112	def
Snoddy	Thomas		1792	1	
Snuffer	John	4	1801	183	juror
Solomon	John	8	1797	85	juror
Spadden	John		1792	6	juror
Spadden	John	5	1794	27	juror
Spadden	Wm	5	1795	44	juror
Spence	Wm	2	1793	110	juror
Spurgeon	Wm	8	1794	33	juror
Stanbaugh	Jacob	11	1795	53	juror

JEFFERSON COUNTY TENNESSEE COURT MINUTE BOOKS
INDEX 1783-1816

LAST	FIRST	MON	YEAR	PAGE	OTHER
Stanbaugh	Jacob	7	1802	208	misdemeanor
Stanbaugh	Jacob	7	1802	208	overseer
Starnes	Nicholas		1792	2	def
Stephenson	Edward	4	1802	201	trespass
Stephenson	Robert	4	1801	183	juror
Sterling	John	8	1794	30	juror
Sterling	John Jr.	1	1798	106	juror
Stewart	Joseph	8	1796	64	juror
Stidham	John	11	1797	99	juror
Stirling	James	1	1802	199	juror
Stirling	John	5	1794	29	juror
Stirling	John Jr.	1	1798	107	juror
Stockdon	Sam	8	1794	31	juror
Stockton	Meshack	7	1800	169	plt
Stoneman	John	11	1797	104	plt
Stout	Jacob	7	1798	123	plt
Stover	Ab.	4	1800	164	witness
Stuart	David		1792	3	
Stuart	David		1792	7	juror
Stuart	David	8	1795	49	juror
Stuart	David	5	1796	60	plt
Stuart	David	1	1799	133	plt
Stuart	Joseph	8	1796	65	juror
Stuart	Joseph	8	1796	65	plt
Stuart	Thomas	11	1796	69	juror
Stuart	Thomas	8	1797	85	juror
Sullens	Joseph	4	1799	139	juror
Sullivan	James	8	1795	49	juror
Surossett	Samuel	11	1797	102	def
Sutherland	David	5	1797	77	juror
Swagerty	Abraham	7	1799	156	def
Swainey	Moses	7	1802	206	juror
Swaly	Jacob	1	1800	159	juror
Swan	Samuel	1	1800	159	juror
Swingle	George	8	1795	51	def
Swingle	George	11	1795	54	def
Swingle	George	8	1797	88	juror
Swingle	George	8	1797	89	victum
Swingle	George	1	1798	110	def

LAST	FIRST	MON	YEAR	PAGE	OTHER
Swingle	George	4	1798	119	plt
Swingle	George	10	1798	128	plt
Swingle	George	7	1799	151	juror
Swingle	George	7	1799	154	plt
Swingle	George	4	1801	183	def
Swingle	George	4	1802	200	def
Swingle	George	7	1802	206	def
Swingle	Michael		1792	7	def
Symon	Robert	5	1797	80	juror
Tabb	Wm	7	1798	125	def
Taft	Peter	5	1797	82	juror
Taft	Peter	8	1797	87	juror
Taft	Peter	1	1798	106	juror
Taft	Peter	1	1798	109	juror
Talbot	Parry	7	1799	149	juror
Talbot	Perry	7	1798	123	juror
Talbott	Mary	1	1802	197	witness
Talbott	Parry	7	1799	153	juror
Talbott	Parry	1	1801	177	juror
Talbott	Parry	7	1801	193	juror
Talbott	Perry	1	1802	197	witness
Talbott	Thomas		1792	7	plt
Taylor	David	8	1795	49	juror
Taylor	James	7	1799	142	plt
Taylor	James	7	1799	153	juror
Taylor	James	1	1802	196	juror
Taylor	John		1792	7	juror
Taylor	John		1792	8	juror
Taylor	John		1792	9	juror
Taylor	John	8	1794	34	juror
Taylor	John	8	1794	34	juror
Taylor	John	8	1794	35	juror
Taylor	John	2	1795	37	robery
Taylor	John	11	1796	69	juror
Taylor	John	4	1801	183	juror
Taylor	Parmenas	11	1795	56	plt
Taylor	Robert	5	1795	46	larceny
Tell	Moses	7	1800	166	juror
Tell	Moses	7	1800	167	plt

JEFFERSON COUNTY TENNESSEE COURT MINUTE BOOKS
INDEX 1783-1816

LAST	FIRST	MON	YEAR	PAGE	OTHER
Terry	Clement	4	1801	183	juror
Terry	Clement	7	1801	193	plt
Terry	Clement	1	1802	199	plt
Tharp	John	8	1797	89	juror
Tharp	John	1	1798	107	juror
Tharp	John	7	1798	122	juror
Tharp	John	7	1798	123	juror
Tharp	John	7	1798	124	juror
Thomas	Wm	11	1797	99	juror
Thomas	Wm	7	1798	123	juror
Thornberry	Ben	5	1795	43	juror
Thornberry	Ben	8	1795	49	juror
Thornberry	Ben	8	1796	63	juror
Thornberry	Ben	1	1798	108	juror
Thornberry	Ben	1	1798	109	juror
Thornberry	Ben	7	1799	156	juror
Thornberry	Ben	1	1801	176	juror
Thornberry	Ben	1	1801	177	juror
Thornberry	Benjamin	1	1798	107	juror
Thornberry	Henry	4	1801	180	juror
Thornberry	Henry Jr.	4	1801	180	juror
Thornberry	Joseph	5	1794	29	juror
Thornberry	Joseph	8	1794	31	juror
Thornberry	Joseph	8	1794	32	juror
Thornberry	Joseph	8	1794	33	juror
Thornberry	Walter	1	1801	176	juror
Thornberry	Walter	1	1801	177	juror
Thornberry	Walter	4	1801	180	juror
Thornbrugh	Ben	5	1796	62	juror
Thornbrugh	Ben	1	1798	106	juror
Thornbury	Joseph	8	1794	30	juror
Thornton	Clark		1792	7	juror
Thornton	Clark		1792	8	juror
Thorp	John	2	1797	75	juror
Thorp	John	8	1797	87	juror
Thrift	William	5	1796	57	def
Todd	James		1792	4	
Todd	James		1792	5	juror
Todd	James		1792	6	juror

LAST	FIRST	MON	YEAR	PAGE	OTHER
Todd	James		1792	18	juror
Todd	James		1792	19	def
Todd	James		1792	21	juror
Todd	James	2	1793	110	juror
Todd	James	2	1795	36	robery
Todd	James	2	1795	42	juror
Todd	James	11	1795	52	juror
Todd	James	5	1796	57	juror
Todd	James	5	1797	77	juror
Todd	James	5	1797	78	juror
Todd	James	5	1797	81	juror
Todd	James	5	1797	84	juror
Todd	James	8	1797	86	juror
Todd	James	8	1797	89	juror
Todd	James	8	1797	91	plt
Todd	James	11	1797	93	juror
Todd	James	11	1797	95	juror
Todd	James	11	1797	96	juror
Todd	James	1	1798	107	juror
Todd	James	1	1798	107	def
Todd	James	1	1798	108	juror
Todd	James	1	1798	108	trespass
Todd	James	1	1798	115	plt
Todd	James	4	1798	120	plt
Todd	James	4	1798	120	plt
Todd	James	7	1798	124	plt
Todd	James	4	1799	135	plt
Todd	James	7	1799	142	def
Todd	James	7	1799	144	def
Todd	James	7	1799	155	def
Todd	James	1	1800	159	def
Todd	James	7	1800	172	def
Todd	John		1792	5	juror
Todd	John		1792	6	juror
Todd	John		1792	18	juror
Todd	John	11	1797	99	plt
Todd	John	11	1797	100	plt
Todd	John	1	1798	110	juror
Todd	John	1	1798	111	juror

LAST	FIRST	MON	YEAR	PAGE	OTHER
Todd	John	1	1798	112	juror
Todd	John	7	1799	151	def
Todd	John	1	1800	159	def
Todd	Low		1792	6	juror
Todd	Low		1792	8	juror
Todd	Low		1792	21	juror
Todd	Low		1792	22	juror
Todd	Low	5	1794	27	juror
Todd	Low	5	1794	29	juror
Todd	Low	8	1795	48	juror
Todd	Low	8	1795	49	juror
Todd	Low	8	1795	51	juror
Todd	Low	11	1795	53	juror
Todd	Low	11	1796	69	juror
Todd	Low	2	1797	70	juror
Todd	Low	2	1797	71	juror
Todd	Low	2	1797	74	juror
Todd	Low	5	1797	84	juror
Todd	Low	1	1798	110	juror
Todd	Low	1	1798	111	juror
Todd	Low	1	1798	112	juror
Todd	Low	4	1799	136	juror
Todd	Low	7	1799	149	juror
Todd	Low	7	1799	150	plt
Trotter	Ellizabeth	10	1798	130	def
Trotter	James	7	1799	149	juror
Trotter	Samuel	7	1799	157	def
Trotter	Wm	1	1798	106	juror
Tucker	Robert	4	1798	119	def
Tully	Charles		1792	19	juror
Turman	Elizabeth	8	1794	32	victum
Turman	Igantius		1792	23	juror
Turman	Ignatius		1792	5	juror
Turman	Ignatius		1792	18	juror
Turman	Ignatius		1792	23	juror
Turman	Ignatius	2	1793	110	def
Turman	Ignatius	2	1795	41	def
Turman	Ignatius	2	1795	42	def
Turman	James		1792	3	

LAST	FIRST	MON	YEAR	PAGE	OTHER
Turman	James		1792	6	def
Turman	James		1792	7	def
Turman	James		1792	12	juror
Turman	James		1792	13	victum
Turman	James		1792	14	juror
Turman	James		1792	15	def
Turman	James		1792	16	def
Turman	James		1792	19	juror
Turman	James		1792	23	plt
Turman	James		1792	23	plt
Turman	James	5	1794	29	def
Turman	James	8	1794	30	plt
Turman	James	8	1794	34	def
Turman	James	5	1797	77	adm.-plt
Turman	James	5	1797	77	adm.-def
Turner	James	1	1798	115	def
Turner	James	4	1799	135	def
Turner	James	4	1799	135	juror
Turner	James	4	1802	202	juror
Turner	John	7	1800	172	juror
Turnley	George	7	1799	155	juror
Turnley	George	7	1801	187	juror
Van Dyke	Freeman	4	1799	138	juror
Van Hooser	Abraham	7	1798	123	juror
Van Hooser	Abraham	10	1798	126	juror
Van Hooser	John		1792	3	
Van Hooser	John		1792	16	juror
Van Hooser	John		1792	17	juror
Van Hooser	John		1792	24	juror
Van Hooser	Valentine	8	1794	33	plt
Van Hoover	Jacob		1792	2	
Vaughn	William		1792	9	juror
Vickers	James	8	1794	33	def
Vickers	James	11	1797	95	plt
Vineyard	George		1792	22	juror
Walker	James	8	1794	33	juror
Walker	James	8	1795	49	juror
Walker	James	11	1795	54	juror
Walker	John	8	1796	64	def

LAST	FIRST	MON	YEAR	PAGE	OTHER
Wall	George	7	1798	121	juror
Wall	George	7	1798	125	def
Wallace	Ben	5	194	28	juror
Wallace	Ben		1792	20	juror
Wallace	Ben M.	5	1794	26	juror
Wallace	Benjamin		1792	20	def
Wallace	Benjamin		1792	23	juror
Wallace	Benjamin M.	8	1794	30	def
Wallace	Jesse	5	1797	84	juror
Wallace	John		1792	20	juror
Wallace	Matthew		1792	20	juror
Wallace	Sam	5	1796	59	juror
Waller	Pleasant	8	1795	51	juror
Walter	Thomas	2	1795	38	juror
Walters	Thomas		1792	15	juror
Walters	Thomas	2	1795	41	juror
Walters	Thomas	2	1795	42	juror
Warren	Robert	4	1798	118	def
Watson	Wm	5	1797	78	juror
Watson	Wm	5	1797	79	juror
Watson	Wm	5	1797	80	juror
Watson	Wm	5	1797	82	juror
Watson	Wm	8	1797	90	juror
Wear	Sam	5	1797	78	plt
Weaver	Adam	4	1802	201	juror
Weaver	George	8	1795	50	juror
Webb	Jeremiah	8	1794	34	juror
Webb	Jeremiah	8	1794	35	juror
Webb	Marady	1	1798	112	juror
Webb	Marida	1	1798	113	juror
Webb	Wm	5	1797	81	def
Webb	Wm	4	1799	138	juror
Welch	Daniel	8	1797	86	plt
Welch	John		1792	6	def
Welch	John	1	1800	160	def
Welch	Thomas		1792	7	juror
Welch	Thomas		1792	10	juror
Welch	Thomas		1792	16	juror
Wells	William	5	1794	25	plt

LAST	FIRST	MON	YEAR	PAGE	OTHER
Wells	Wm	7	1798	125	def
West	Edward Samuel	4	1798	119	def
West	Sam	1	1798	115	juror
West	Sam	1	1800	159	juror
West	Thomas		1792	15	juror
West	Thomas		1792	24	juror
West	Thomas	5	1794	27	def
West	Thomas	5	1794	29	juror
West	Thomas	8	1794	30	juror
West	Thomas	2	1795	37	juror
White	John	5	1795	46	juror
White	John	5	1797	78	plt
White	Sam	1	1802	199	juror
White	Thomas		1792	9	juror
White	Thomas		1792	11	juror
White	Wercley	5	1794	29	juror
White	Wertley	5	1797	81	juror
White	Wesley	8	1794	30	juror
White	Wesley	11	1796	68	juror
White	Wesley	5	1797	78	juror
White	William	5	1794	25	juror
White	William	10	1798	126	larceny
White	Wm	5	1796	62	def
Whiteside	Francis	11	1795	55	plt
Whittles	Levi	11	1797	95	juror
Wier	Sam	11	1795	54	juror
Wilcockson	George	11	1795	54	juror
Wilcockson	George	11	1795	56	juror
Wilcockson	George	5	1796	60	juror
Wilcockson	George	2	1797	75	juror
Wilcockson	George	7	1798	124	juror
Wilhite	Matthias	11	1795	56	juror
Wilhoit	Julius		1792	7	juror
Wilhoit	Julius		1792	8	juror
Willcockson	George	11	1795	53	juror
Willcox	Ben	5	1794	25	juror
Willcox	James	5	1794	25	juror
Willcox	James	5	1794	27	juror
Williams	Allen		1792	9	juror

LAST	FIRST	MON	YEAR	PAGE	OTHER
Williams	Allen		1792	11	juror
Williams	Allen	11	1795	52	juror
Williams	Allen	5	1796	57	juror
Williams	Allen	5	1796	58	juror
Williams	Arthur	11	1797	97	juror
Williams	Arthur	11	1797	98	victum
Williams	Ezekiel		1792	12	juror
Williams	Ezekiel		1792	14	juror
Williams	Flippia		1792	2	
Williams	James	7	1799	157	larceny
Williams	Joseph	4	1799	136	juror
Williams	Littleton	4	1800	163	juror
Williams	Lydia	5	1796	59	plt
Williams	Wm	4	1800	164	juror
Willson	Adam		1792	15	juror
Willson	Adam		1792	16	juror
Willson	Adam		1792	18	juror
Willson	Adam	8	1794	33	juror
Willson	Adam	5	1795	43	juror
Willson	Adam	8	1796	64	juror
Willson	Adam	8	1796	64	juror
Willson	Adam	11	1796	68	juror
Willson	Adam	8	1797	92	def
Willson	Daniel	8	1797	88	juror
Willson	Jacob	1	1800	159	juror
Willson	James		1792	16	juror
Willson	James	8	1794	30	juror
Willson	John		1792	22	juror
Willson	John		1792	23	juror
Willson	John	11	1797	96	victum
Willson	John	11	1797	97	A & B
Willson	John	1	1798	106	juror
Willson	John	4	1799	139	juror
Willson	Joseph	1	1802	196	juror
Willson	Joseph	4	1802	201	juror
Willson	Robert	8	1795	51	juror
Willson	William	8	1795	51	juror
Willson	William	4	1799	136	juror
Willson	Wm	8	1797	85	juror

LAST	FIRST	MON	YEAR	PAGE	OTHER
Willson	Wm	8	1797	88	juror
Willson	Wm	1	1798	115	juror
Willson	Wm	4	1798	117	juror
Willson	Wm	7	1798	121	juror
Willson	Wm	4	1799	138	juror
Willson	Wm	1	1801	176	juror
Willson	Wm	1	1801	177	juror
Willson	Wm	7	1801	192	juror
Willson	Wm	4	1802	201	juror
Wilson	Adam		1792	14	juror
Wilson	Adam		1792	15	juror
Winton	Wm	7	1799	156	juror
Witson	James	10	1800	174	witness
Witt	Ayers	1	1801	178	juror
Witt	Ayers	4	1801	181	witness
Witt	Caleb	1	1799	132	juror
Witt	Caleb	7	1799	141	juror
Witt	Caleb	7	1799	142	juror
Witt	Elijah		1792	4	
Witt	Elijah	4	1800	163	def
Witt	Joseph		1792	2	
Witt	Joseph		1792	7	juror
Witt	Joseph		1792	16	juror
Witt	Joseph		1792	17	juror
Witt	Joseph		1792	24	juror
Witt	Joseph	4	1799	135	juror
Witt	Joseph	4	1799	138	juror
Witt	Joseph	4	1801	181	larceny
Witt	Joseph	4	1802	200	juror
Witt	Jospeh	4	1802	202	juror
Witt	Thomas		1792	22	juror
Woodard	Abraham	5	1794	29	juror
Woodard	Abraham	8	1794	30	juror
Woodard	Abraham	8	1794	31	juror
Woodard	Abraham	8	1794	33	juror
Woodward	Aaron	1	1800	159	juror
Work	Robert	1	1798	113	plt
Wright	Edward		1792	16	juror
Wright	Edward		1792	17	juror

LAST	FIRST	MON	YEAR	PAGE	OTHER
Wright	Edward	5	1796	62	juror
Wright	Edward	8	1796	63	juror
Wright	Isaac	1	1801	178	def
Wright	Isaac	4	1801	183	def
Wright	John	11	1795	52	juror
Wright	John	5	1796	57	juror
Wright	John	5	1796	58	juror
Wright	John	5	1796	62	juror
Wright	John	8	1796	63	juror
Wright	John	7	1798	124	juror
Wright	John	10	1798	127	juror
Wright	John	4	1802	200	juror
Wright	Joshua	11	1797	99	juror
Wright	Joshua	1	1798	106	juror
Wright	Joshua	1	1798	107	juror
Wright	Joshua	1	1798	108	juror
Wright	Joshua	1	1798	109	juror
Wright	Joshua	10	1798	126	juror
Wright	Joshua	10	1798	127	juror
Yancey	Ambrose		1792	19	juror
Yancey	Ambrose		1792	20	juror
Yancey	Ambrose		1792	20	juror
Yell ?	Moses	11	1797	97	juror